VISUAL STRATEGIES FOR IMPROVING COMMUNICATION

Volume 1: PRACTICAL SUPPORTS FOR SCHOOL AND HOME

Linda A. Hodgdon, M.ED., CCC-SLP

QUIRKROBERTS PUBLISHING

© 1995
Second Printing, 1996
Third Printing, 1997
Fourth Printing, 1997
Fifth Printing, 1998
Sixth Printing, 1998
Seventh Printing, 1999

QuirkRoberts Publishing
P.O. Box 71
Troy, Michigan 48099-0071
Telephone: (248) 879-2598
Fax: (248) 879-2599

Original Illustrations: Rachel Hopkins.
Book Design: Frank Slanczka.

Cow illustration: Joseph Anderson, (page 184) reprinted with permission from
Imaginart International, Inc., Bisbee, AZ.

Kmart logo and photo are used with permission: Kmart Corporation, Troy, MI.
Campbell's logo used with permission: Campbell's, Camden, NJ.
McDonald's logo and photos used with permission: McDonalds, Oakbrook, IL.

SnackWells, Honey Maid, and RITZ are registered trademarks of Nabisco Foods
Group, used with permission: Nabisco Foods Group, Parsippany, NJ.

Picture Communication Symbols (pages 31, 54, 110, 163, 164) used with
permission: Mayer-Johnson Co., P.O. Box 1579, Solana Beach, CA 92075

ISBN: 0-9616786-1-5
Library of Congress Catalog Card Number: 94-68080

This book is dedicated to the staff, students and families in the Macomb Intermediate School District Autistic Program who have enthusiastically supported the development of visual strategies.

I hear and I forget.

I see and I remember.

I do and I understand.

Chinese Proverb

Table of Contents

Foreword

Perhaps some of the greatest strides in communication intervention for persons with moderate and severe communication disorders have derived from the increased understanding of the unique patterns of learning associated with the syndrome of autism. A substantial amount of research has shown that persons with autism demonstrate information processing characterized by strengths in wholistic, gestalt processing. This processing strength is well suited to the comprehension of spatially organized, non transient information. The weaknesses associated with this learning style involve processing analytic sequential information. This results in difficulties in understanding temporally organized, transient information. (Prizant & Schuler, 1987).

The evidence of this unique learning style has led to greater understanding of the communication and language problems associated with autism and other disabilities characterized by severe language/communication impairments. Greater understanding has led to enormous strides in devising communication intervention approaches and strategies that have resulted in the development of effective communication skills for persons with autism and other challenging conditions.

In Visual Strategies for Improving Communication, Linda Hodgdon presents a multitude of practical applications of the communication intervention strategies firmly grounded in learning style research and years of experience serving as a communication specialist for students with autism. Hers is a "how to" book, a manual designed to assist parents, teachers, speech-language pathologists and others to devise solutions to the communication and self management challenges that are common to autism and other conditions involving severe communication disorders. This book is chock full of examples and illustrations, providing clear guidance and direction to all who wish to employ effective strategies to improve communication skills. Every strategy and example has been tested in Hodgdon's clinical and teaching experience, and has proven effectiveness.

Hodgdon's approach to "Visually Mediated Communication" strategies is unique in many respects. In marked contrast to many communication intervention programs for persons with autism which focus primarily on expressive communication, Hodgdon's initial and primary intervention concern is comprehension - comprehension of the environment, comprehension of requests and directions, comprehension of people and language. The effectiveness of her strategies for fostering comprehension is a key factor accounting for the success of her entire communication intervention program.

Many persons with autism and other disabilities experience profound difficulties in comprehension, especially language comprehension, due to their unique learning style. By insuring comprehension of the environment, expectations, and others, the foundation for the development of expressive communications skills is established.

Another unique aspect of Hodgdon's intervention is her presentation of "Visually Mediated Communication" strategies as physical "tools," supports or mediators for internal psychological processes, such as language, memory, planning, and self control. Her approach is consistent with Vygotsky's theory of self regulation of behavior (i.e., self direction, self determination). In Vygotsky's theory, language is the primary tool, first used by others to guide and mediate the thinking and behavior of the child, and eventually used by the child in "inner speech" to guide his or her own behavior, and problem solving. (Vygotsky, 1978). For persons for whom language does not readily function as a tool (due to learning style differences), other mediating tools must be employed that eventually lead to self regulation of thinking and behavior. The strategies Hodgdon describes clearly exemplify the movement from physical (visual) to psychological tools, and from other regulation to self regulation of behavior and thinking.

Firmly grounded in theory and research, Hodgdon's book is unique in the sheer volume of intervention suggestions, examples and illustrations it contains. It is well organized, easy to follow, and reader friendly with its question-answer dialogue format. This book is a "must have" for all persons who wish to foster better communication with and by persons with autism, and it is a"gift" for communication specialists working with any students having moderate to severe language and communication problems.

Kathleen S. Pistono, Ph.D.
   Consultant for Speech and Language Impaired
   Macomb Intermediate School District
   Clinton Township, Michigan

References:

Prizant, B. M., & Schuler, A. L. (1987). Facilitating communication: Language approaches. In D. Cohen and A. Donnellan (Eds.), Handbook of autism and pervasive developmental disorders (pp. 316-332). New York: Wiley.

Vygotsky, L. S. (1987). Mind in society: The development of higher psychological processes. Cambridge: Harvard University Press.

Introduction

This book is a collection of practical ideas and techniques: how some educators have taken sound theory and research, added a dash of creative experimenting, and translated it into meaningful training and programming tools for students who experience moderate to severe communication disabilities. This information has evolved as the result of years of working with students who experience disabilities such as Autism, Emotional Impairments, Learning Disorders, Attention Deficit Disorders, and Cognitive Impairments.

When we take on the task of working with students who learn differently, our most familiar teaching strategies and goals are put to the test. Students *can* learn. The question is *what* and *how*. Our responsibility as professionals or parents is, in part, one of "discovering" them. What does he like? What is she interested in? What does he want or not want? Most importantly, we need to discover *how* he learns; *how* she understands. That is the key.....to determine what is inside, hidden behind a veil of behaviors and perceptual handicaps, and to discover how to reach it effectively. This discovery process has revealed a large group of students who understand what they *see* better than what they *hear.*

It is through this discovery process that the concept of using **Visually Supported Communication** or **Visually Mediated Communication** strategies has evolved and developed. Success has built upon success. As one student or teacher has benefited from one idea, the challenge has been to develop a second and a third. Over a period of several years the results have been dramatic. Testimonials from school staff and parents have supported the direction enthusiastically.

In spite of what the adults have to say, student response is the real test of meaningfulness. Confirmation of the value of visual tools comes when students respond to them and use them. Just watching someone like Jay, a student who was normally oblivious to the daily routine, rush into the classroom to go look at the daily schedule to find out what is happening today is enough to realize there is value in this concept. The day she pulled out her rule page to tell another student to be quiet, Clara reached a new level of communication. When Ronny observed that some of his classmates had visual tools to organize themselves, he asked the teacher if he could have some "special pictures" too. Jay, Clara, Ronny and other students like them experience an improved quality of life as the result of integrating visual supports into their communication systems.

It is not unusual for students who experience severe communication disorders to demonstrate fragmented skills and inconsistent performance. The ideas in this book suggest a shift in focus, or at least a broadened perspective, from some of the typical educational programming for them. There is a tendency to focus communication training on developing student's *expressive* communication skills; providing strategies to help the student to communicate information to others. ***Visually Mediated Communication*** is a collection of tools and ideas that shift the focus toward enhancing the student's *receptive* ability; supporting the student's attempts to understand and interpret information. This focus leads to greater comprehension, which leads to greater involvement and participation, which ultimately leads to more effective expression. The visual tools support communication by mediating the communication process between students and the rest of their world.

Many people use a few of these ideas...few people use many of them.

Expanding the use of visual strategies is a needed dimension in educational programming. Many people may already use a few visual strategies; few people use many of them. Introducing these concepts results in positive, frequently dramatic, changes in student performance. Initially developed with targeted students with autism, these techniques have generated substantial enthusiasm among professionals working with students in a variety of settings and with a variety of learning needs.

This is not a curriculum, however, these tools and strategies will support any well thought out functional curriculum. Some of the strategies that are suggested do not follow the traditional teaching methods common in our educational environments. The reasons for these will be explored. There is no specific developmental order to be followed. Rather, decisions about what to use or try with a particular student should be based on individual needs and abilities demonstrated. Some suggestions will be made regarding considerations when making those decisions.

The development of visual tools is not a behavior program by itself. The tools discussed can support many well thought out behavior programs. There are many cases documented where the use of visual tools has given students such strong communication and environmental support that the need for other behavior programs has been reduced or eliminated. Developing visual tools to accompany a behavior plan can help guide the plan design and clarify the specifics for student success.

This book is by no means all inclusive. It is just a beginning. Hopefully these ideas will stimulate more of your own. The best resources are not the ones to reproduce on the photocopy machine, but the ones that stimulate creative solutions to unique individual needs.

Now the challenge: Consider yourself embarking on a journey that will have many interesting and challenging visual stops along the way. It is an endless journey. There will always be more opportunities for the application of visual tools.

Part 1

INTRODUCTION TO VISUALLY MEDIATED COMMUNICATION

Chapter I

What Is Visually Mediated Communication?

Effective communication does not just happen. It takes considerable effort from both the sender and the receiver of information to ensure that communication attempts accomplish their intent. Those who experience communication disorders encounter exceptional difficulty participating in the communication process. Fortunately, employing visual aids to support the communication process can significantly improve their successful participation.

What are visual supports?

Visual supports are those things we *see* that enhance the communication process. Ranging from body movements to environmental cues, visual supports capitalize on a person's ability to gain information from the sense of sight. Visual supports are an integral part of the communication circle, enhancing effective receiving, processing, action and expression. Efficient use of visual supports is a critical part of a person's communication system. Visual supports include the following forms:

1. Body Language
2. Natural Environmental Cues
3. Traditional Tools for Organization and Giving Information
4. Specially Designed Tools to Meet Specific Needs

Body Language

The communication message is greatly affected by the use of natural and formalized body movements to communicate messages and clarify communication. They include:

- facial expressions
- body orientation and proximity
- body stance
- movement of body
- reaching, touching, pointing
- eye contact, eye gaze, gaze shift

The ability to interpret and use natural body signals significantly affects the effectiveness of the communication message.

Natural Environmental Cues

The environment naturally contains an abundance of visual information. Consider:

- furniture arrangement
- location and movement of people and objects
- printed material such as signs, signals, logos, labels, prices
- written messages, instructions, choices, menus
- directions on packages, machines, or in business locations

It is critical to be able to interpret the meaning of those things that we see in the environment to help us function effectively and independently.

Traditional Tools for Organization and Giving Information

Most people access or develop a variety of visual supports to help organize their lives. Think how you use:

- calendars, daily planners
- schedules, TV guides, theater guides
- shopping lists, notes, menus
- signs, labels
- maps
- checkbooks, telephone books
- assembly or operating instructions

Teaching the use of these common forms of visual tools can be a valuable part of the communication information system for students with communication impairments. Frequently, these students need to be specifically taught to access information that other students learn to use more incidentally.

Specially Designed Tools to Meet Specific Needs

Many individualized tools can be designed to give the structure and information necessary to handle specific problems or situations. Some are variations of natural environment or traditional tools and others are unique designs developed to accomplish an identified need. Chapters 2, 3, 4, and 5 will provide details for many specially designed options.

I never thought about how much we use visual information. Is that what this book is all about?

Yes, the primary focus of this book will be on exploring the development and use of environmental, traditional, and specially designed visual tools to improve communication.

Assessment guidelines and training suggestions are offered to provide a framework for making decisions about implementing these strategies. An endless variety of visual supports can become part of a student's program, limited only by need and imagination. The implementation of visual strategies should be considered as a part of any student's well-designed communication system.

Who is this book for?

The strategies presented here will help those who live with or work with students who experience moderate to severe communication handicaps. Speech-Language Pathologists, classroom teachers, other educators, parents, and other caregivers will find useful information. Consultants, supervisors, and those who plan curriculum and programming can find application.

These ideas have many practical uses, not only in special education environments, but in regular education settings as well. Many of the strategies discussed have *application for all students*, not just those with special needs. As programming options such as inclusion and mainstreaming dominate the educational horizon, educational environments for students (and educators) will undergo change. The use of visual communication strategies can and should be considered as a viable means to enhance these settings. As a student's life crosses several environments, collaboration among the various people and environments will only enhance the success of the systems.

Visual tools provide the support necessary to raise students to increased levels of participation and independence. Consequently, this book is for anyone who is facing the challenge of developing meaningful educational programming for students of varying needs.

Students who benefit from visual supports to improve communication include those who have received diagnoses such as:
- *Autism*
- *Aphasia*
- *Attention Deficit Disorder*
- *Behavior Disorder*
- *Bilingual*
- *Central Processing Disorder*
- *Cognitive Impairment*
- *Dyslexia*
- *Emotional Impairment*
- *Fragile X*
- *Learning Disability*
- *Language Delay*
- *Language Disorder*
- *Mental Impairment*
- *Pervasive Developmental Disorder*
- *Traumatic Brain Injury*
- *And More*

Do not assume visual supports are useful only for non-verbal students

For the purposes of easy reading, this book frequently uses the word "teacher" to represent the student's communication partner or caregiver, whoever that is. Although a majority of the examples evolve around school environments, any of these strategies can be developed or adapted for any environment the student is in.

Who is this programming for?

Do not discount these strategies because your students have not received a diagnosis of autism. What we have learned with one group of students is increasing our understanding about the learning styles of many of those who experience communication and learning difficulties. Students may demonstrate this learning style even if they have not been specifically diagnosed.

- Preschool
- Kindergarten
- Elementary
- Middle School
- High School
- Adult

Originally these *Visually Mediated Communication* strategies were developed as part of the communication programming for students who experience autism. It was observed that many of the students who receive that diagnosis demonstrated behavioral characteristics that appeared directly related to their communication abilities and inabilities. In an attempt to assist the students in their educational performances, a variety of visual tools and strategies were added to their programming. Most of these students demonstrated improved understanding and participation when their environments were enriched visually.

As the visual techniques have been disseminated, application has been found for many other students. Those with virtually every disability label (except blind), including those who seem to defy traditional diagnostic descriptions, have demonstrated positive response to visual supports. The techniques are working their way into preschools, kindergartens, and many regular education classrooms in various forms. Through consultation designed to prepare classroom environments for the inclusion of students with special needs, regular education teachers are seeing the relevance of these strategies for all of their students.

My students are all verbal. Will they benefit from visual tools?

It does not matter if a student is verbal or nonverbal. Although visual tools can help students express themselves better, their primary purpose is to enhance student understanding.

Do not assume that a student understands because he talks.

You are describing many students who can benefit. Are there any others?

Don't forget to reevaluate the students who are described like this:

> *"He understands everything I say."*
> ❊
> *"He is too high skilled for that."*
> ❊
> *"He is too low skilled for that."*
> ❊
> *"He already knows that."*
> ❊
> *"He wouldn't use them."*
> ❊
> *"He understands; he is just being bad"*
> ❊
> *"He knows what I want; he is just not paying attention"*

It is common to *assume* that students are comprehending and organizing more auditory information than they actually do. Their performance irregularities are then attributed to behavior or effort. Frequently, students who have earned diagnoses that suggest emotional or behavioral problems are described in those terms. Many students from these groups have demonstrated improved performance using visual tools to assist in various areas of their lives. Do not eliminate them from consideration.

Think of it like this: The use of *Visual Communication Strategies* acknowledges the strengths and more proficient skill areas of many students and develops aids and systems to assist them in using their stronger skills to overcome or circumvent some of their areas of difficulty.

Autism is a "low incidence" disorder. A comparatively small number of students with special needs receive that diagnosis. There is currently an increasing number of students that are identified as the medical and educational communities continue to modify the definition. Few educators are specifically trained to educate these students. In fact, many professionals report that servicing this population is " less preferred" than many other students with special needs. This results from lack knowledge and experience with that group. When attempting to develop training programs for this population, educators frequently find that the strategies and techniques that have worked for other students do not work. As one develops increased knowledge and communication strategies evolve, what becomes evident is that strategies that work for other students do not necessarily work for students with autism, but strategies that work for students with autism can be wonderfully effective additions to the programming of other students...particularly those who experience some form of communication disorder. By learning how students with autism learn and understand we are learning about other students, too.

Why do you use visual tools?

Because they work! Take the following test to gain a perspective about your own experiences.

VISUAL TOOL MINI TEST

Do you have a **calendar** that you write things on to help you organize your life?

Do you have a **list of "things to do"** on your desk or refrigerator?

Have you ever pointed to a **picture** in an advertisement or a menu to show someone what you want?

Do you make up a **shopping list** before you go to the store?

Do you ever read a **sign** to tell you what line to stand in or what door to exit from?

Have you ever followed a **recipe** in a cookbook to create some delicious dinner entree? Did you go back to that recipe each time you wanted to cook that item?

Do you ever write **notes** to your family members reminding them to do things?

Do you scan the **menu** to evaluate your choices before ordering in a restaurant?

Have you ever made a **check list** for your children to help them remember to brush their teeth?

Did you ever attach a **note** to your bathroom mirror to remind you to do something?

Have you had the experience of assembling a new bicycle by following the **"easy to follow-step by step"** instructions?

If you answered yes to any of the above questions you have used *Visual Communication Tools* to help you organize your life, make a choice, communicate with others, or accomplish a task. We all use them as a part of our daily life.

Recall another experience: when you frequent your favorite fast food restaurant, do you find yourself looking up at the menu or the dessert display to check the choices, even though you already know what you are going to order? Why? What does looking at that menu do for you? You are using the *visual tool* to organize your thinking and affirm your selection.

We commonly use visual supports to organize our lives, get information and communicate. This book is about taking those same kinds of visual tools that we find helpful in everyday life and expanding the concepts for our students. It is about using these aids to mediate or support their communication interactions. It is about using visual supports to help organize their environments and facilitate their learning.

Why is visual communication important?

People who experience autism, who can describe their perceptual reactions to the world, reveal they experience difficulty attending to, modulating, or understanding auditory input. One person described the difficulty she would encounter in some communication settings. For example, a telephone conversation about an object in a different location was significantly more difficult for her than conversing in the location with that object present. She could not understand what was being described to her over the telephone. Once she went to the location to see it, she understood. Others describe their hypersensitivity to sound or their inability to listen selectively.

THINK ABOUT THIS: Our lives are bombarded with visual stimuli. Companies have become sophisticated at designing visual ways to get us to recognize and remember them. We live in environments filled with visual tools to give us information and manipulate our actions. We gravitate to television; a visual medium.

Imagine what it feels like trying to listen to the championship ball game on the radio when the reception is awful. Another station keeps surfacing and the static is so loud that you can barely decipher what the announcer says. You have to lean toward the radio, close your eyes, and silence everyone around you while you strain to hear what is happening. Could this be even vaguely similar to the experience of students who have difficulty attending and comprehending auditory messages?

Another person experienced difficulty answering questions that were not written down. Still another described how difficult it is to attend to a conversation when there is background noise. If there is something to look at, it is easier to focus on the conversation. What they are really telling us is:

That statement holds true for *most* of our students who experience autism...and many of our other students with special needs...and other people who identify themselves as being visual learners.

Think about how many of those under our educational care display behaviors that earn descriptions such as: auditory impairment, distractible, attention deficit disorder, hyperactive, auditory processing problems, auditory memory deficit, etc., etc. For various reasons they have auditory disturbances, yet they live and learn in environments that are primarily auditory. The most common way people communicate to these students is through the auditory channel. At the same time many of these students display relative strengths in visual skills. In fact, many of them have been observed to have visual memory or visual interpretation skills that appear far superior to their auditory performance. Why not maximize that strength?

Do you have an answering machine? Isn't it sometimes a challenge to decipher messages? What happens when people leave lots of specific information like names and addresses and phone numbers? Isn't it nice to be able to replay that tape several times to get the details? Think about how life and school routines don't easily provide instant replays.

Why are visual messages easier to understand than auditory messages?

For a part of the answer, think about your own experience in this type of situation:

Have you ever gone to one of those nicer dining establishments where the waiter hands you a menu and then verbally tells you the six specials of the day in rapid succession (baked scrod ala orange...,etc.,etc.)? Given that situation, a very large percentage of people will listen to the specials and then ask to have the details repeated several times. That verbal menu was a *transient* message. It was difficult to process and difficult to remember because it came and went so quickly.

You may prefer to ignore the specials and look at the menu to order something from what is printed on it. You can read through the choices, go back to the beginning again, and look around as much as you need to make the selection. The words and pictures on that menu remain in place as long as necessary for the decision to be made. In addition, if the menu is in French and you can't pronounce the name, you can point to your choice and the waiter will know what you want. The written menu is a *non-transient* message. It remains fixed until you can accomplish your purpose with the information.

There is evidence that students who experience auditory processing problems have difficulty processing rapidly changing acoustic information. That means the brief cues and rapid rates of the normal speech message present a severe challenge to these students. Visual stimuli can provide non-transient messages that exist for the length of time it takes the student to process the information. The visual message accommodates, in part, for the functioning style of these students.

When you say "visual" I think of pictures. Is that what you mean?

The term "visual" includes anything you see. Body language, objects, and printed matter of any kind can become visual supports for communication. These things will not be valuable, however, unless the student can derive meaning from them. Students will realize the greatest benefit from supports that are:

- easily recognized
- easily understood
- universally understood

"Sometimes people would have to repeat a particular sentence several times for me, as I would hear it in bits, and the way in which my mind had segmented their sentence into words left me with a strange and sometimes unintelligible message. It was a bit like when someone plays around with the volume switch on the TV."

Donna Williams
Nobody Nowhere

Did you ever experience this: the radio or television is on as "background noise." All of a sudden you realize they are giving a phone number you need. By the time you hear and pay attention to the information, the speaker has completed that topic and is moving on to something else. There is no opportunity to do "instant replay." Do our students feel like this?

"...my response to what people said to me would often be delayed as my mind had to take time to sort out what they had said. The more stress I was under, the worse it became."

Donna Williams
Nobody Nowhere

Pictures are one of the most universal mediums. Think of how the advertising industry communicates messages to us. They catch our attention very effectively by using liberal doses of color, distinctive logos, photos, drawings, and a comparatively small amount of written text. Why try to reinvent the wheel? Surely the dollars and research that have gone into developing their techniques are not modest.

Choosing the form of a visual support will depend on the student's ability, the environment, and what is available. Chapter 8 will discuss this point in more detail. For now, just remember that any of the visual tools in this book can be developed in a variety of forms. Which form you choose needs to match the student's ability level and what his current educational objectives dictate.

Why do these individuals function better visually?

The process of taking in information, processing it, and making meaning of it for some form of output or response has the potential for breakdown at many stages. There are probably many explanations. Consider these two descriptions to help understand what our targeted student might be experiencing.

1. Difficulty shifting and reestablishing attention
Students with autism experience difficulty smoothly and accurately controlling the shifting and reestablishing of attention. Current research suggests that due to cerebellar deficiencies, their ability to modulate sensory input is affected. The early acquisition of social and communication skills requires the ability to quickly interpret the rapid and dynamic ebb and flow of social interaction. It requires very rapid selection, prioritizing, and processing, of information. The nervous system of these students does not have the capacity to perform this function adequately. Their resulting inability produces, at least in part, the early aloof and non engaged behaviors and the auditory inconsistencies described by researchers of autism. By contrast, these individuals display preference for things that are more invariant or more predictable. [1]

2. Difficulty attending to foreground sounds and blocking out background noises

One other phenomenon has been described. In the typical environment there are many simultaneous sound sources. Intentional communication messages are competing with other choices: doors closing, papers shuffling, and other sounds from the environment. The normal listener is able to focus his attention selectively on the communication message (foreground) while blocking out the background noise. Some listeners, however, are unable to do that. They perceive all auditory information at equal intensity. Their inability to listen selectively results in a "sound reception machine" that is either all on or all off. It is an inefficient system.

Now, recall our discussion of transient vs. non-transient messages. Communication modes such as speech, manual signs, and gestures are transient; they remain present for only a short period of time. Tasks that require the sequential processing of transient information constitute an area of weakness in autism and other communication disorders. These students demonstrate comparative strengths with tasks that involve interpretation of non-transient stimulus (i.e., visual) that is processed in a "gestalt" fashion. The term gestalt suggests interpretation of the message as a whole chunk rather than being subjected to analysis of component parts. [2]

Keeping in mind these styles of interpreting the environment, think about this: Consider the implications for a student who experiences difficulty shifting and reestablishing attention, trying to capture the essence of a transient auditory message in a noisy environment. Add that to the "all-or-nothing" listening style he may experience. Receiving that transient auditory message requires exactly the skills the student experiences difficulty with. The result is an inefficient system for understanding the environment. A spoken message may be completed before the student is focused enough to receive it.

Think about how you are able to focus your attention and block out auditory distractions. For example, can you read or have a conversation with someone while music is playing in the background? Many of our targeted students would not be able to manage those situations successfully.

There is a group of students who learn language differently. They do not follow the normal patterns for interpreting the speech of others or acquiring expressive speech. To them, language occurs in pieces or chunks for certain purposes but they lack the ability to effectively understand more specific word usage and more subtle word and grammatical differences. For example: when someone asks "How are you?" the student answers "fine". If the question changes to "How old are you?" the student response to that may also be "fine". If it is a routine to point to his empty milk carton and tell him to "put it in the wastebasket" he will follow that direction. If your direction changes to "put it on the counter" when you point to it, the carton could end up in the wastebasket. These students are gestalt learners. They learn big "chunks." They do not adequately analyze those big chunks into smaller pieces.

These students may respond adequately to brief phrases or routine directions, however they find it difficult, if not impossible, to understand more complex language. They learn better with visual than with auditory cues. A common teaching technique is to expand language output, using expanded descriptions and directions. This is just the opposite of what these students need.

Expressive communication problems are generally most obvious. Difficulties with attending and processing communication are not as clearly identified. How skillfully a student can use environmental supports will make a difference in his apparent ability with the communication process.

Some students demonstrate what we call "slow processing". It takes longer than normal for them to take in the information, make meaning from it, and then formulate a response. Imagine what happens if constant repetition of the request interrupts that process and results in the student starting from the beginning again each time the process is interrupted.

Conversely, the presentation of visual (non-transient) communication messages provides an opportunity for the child to engage his attention before the message disappears. The stability of the visual message allows the element of time necessary for the student to disengage, shift, and re-engage attention. As a result of this process, many of these students appear to understand what they see better than what they hear. In addition, the visual message remains visible to enable the student to focus on it long enough or return to it as needed to establish memory for the message it is communicating. [3]

When you realize how many of those under our educational care display behaviors that earn descriptions such as auditory impairment, distractible, attention deficit disorder, hyperactive, auditory processing problems, auditory memory deficit, and so on, there are many reasons for disability. Understanding at least a part of why they have difficulty can give some valuable insights for designing training programs. For various reasons they have auditory disturbances, yet they live and learn in environments that are primarily auditory. The most common way people communicate to these students is through the auditory channel. At the same time, many of these students display relative strengths in visual skills. In fact, many of them have been observed to have visual memory or visual interpretation skills that appear far superior to their auditory performance.

Using visual tools to mediate communication interactions and support understanding provides a non-transient foundation essential for more effective communication. It builds on student's strengths rather than placing more demands on their area of greatest difficulty. When visual tools are used to give these students information and directions, student comprehension increases *significantly.* For many individuals with moderate to severe communication difficulties, the use of visually supported communication is more effective and efficient than just talking to them.

This is finally making sense. I am beginning to understand. Are we talking about both my verbal and non verbal students?

It is easy to make a judgement about a student's communication ability by observing his ability to talk, or use other means to express himself. Remember, expression is only one part of the communication cycle.

The use of visual communication tools is not determined by a student's ability to talk. These tools are valuable with both verbal and nonverbal students. Their use is determined in part by the students ability to take in information and make meaning from it.

The suggestion is to refocus attention on *understanding* as it relates to student behavior and learning. The visual communication tools suggested in this book should be viewed as tools to enhance *both* receptive and expressive skills. Many of them are established as receptive tools; tools to give students information. Then as a *secondary* benefit they are used by the student to enhance his expressive attempts.

This book is about recognizing the relative strengths and weaknesses of these students and making adjustments in their communication environments to accommodate for that. It is about using visual tools to mediate and enhance the communication process. It is about creating environments where communication interactions will be more effective and more efficient.

Don't teachers already do this?

When observing educational environments it is common to observe a few visual aids. *Many people use a few visual tools: few people use many.* Few people use the visual tools as consistently and with as much emphasis on integrating them into the fiber of classroom communication as could be done.

> *A student's ability to speak does not determine the need for visual supports. The decision is related to the student's ability to **understand**. Visual aids can be valuable for **both** verbal and non-verbal students.*

> *It is not unusual for people to **assume** students understand more than they actually do. Verbal students who use a lot of echolalia can be particularly deceiving. Just because they can talk, it does not mean they understand everything. Their **appearance** of linguistic capability can distort the perception of their overall communicative ability.*

What about sign language?
Sign language is a visual medium.

I am glad you asked. When the use of visual strategies is mentioned, the topic of sign language generally emerges. After all, sign language is visual.

In the context of this book, the development of visual communication strategies stresses two main goals.

Goal 1: Communicate in a medium that is non-transient.

Remember, the effectiveness of visual supports comes, in large part, because the tools offer a non-transient message that accommodates for the processing time necessary for many students. Manual signing is a transient signal...it moves...it is there, and then it is gone.

Goal 2: Use symbols that are universally understood and quickly recognized by anyone who is using them.

Sign language is not universally understood. In fact, even people who have some training in sign language can become confused by the different sign languages and the inaccurate sign production of students. Although the use of signing has its place in many communication systems, it also has its limitations.

What are the benefits?

Learning manual signs has been the introduction to intentional communication for some students. There are many reports of nonverbal students whose communication worlds have been unlocked through the use of sign. Interestingly, some nonverbal students have begun to talk after being taught to produce manual signs; as if the manual motor movements "prime the pump" for oral motor movement.

From a *receptive* point of view, pairing signs with verbal directions to students is often an effective way of capturing their attention. Compared to other communication tools, your hands are always there; they can't be misplaced. They are not inconvenient to carry around. For those who will be living in an environment where sign is a primary form of communication (i.e., the hearing impaired community) the system offers students who are cognitively capable, the ability to communicate with a sophisticated system.

What are the problems?

Consider the profile of students with communication disorders. Remember, many of them are not able to effectively process transient information. In addition, they may have difficulties in language comprehension, motor planning, attending, understanding abstract representations, memory, and many other supporting skills. As educational programs have promoted the development of manual signing, some of the positive results have been balanced with difficulties.

- Students with motor difficulties are not able to replicate the fine motor movements necessary for many signs.

- Motor and memory difficulties result in students producing their own personal versions of signs.

- Many students are not able to effectively interpret the subtle differences in signs if introduced to too many.

- Those students who learn larger sign vocabularies may actually be able to effectively use them with fewer people because the people they are communicating with don't know their vocabulary.

- Students who have a non-transient, gestalt, concrete learning style are trying to learn a transient, analytical, abstract system.

- Sign language is not a universally understood system. Everyone does not know sign-particularly in the community outside the school environment.

Does that mean I shouldn't use signs?

No, but it means that it is necessary to plan a student's communication system carefully so it will work well for him. If using signs is a consideration for part of a student's communication system the selection should be balanced with the need for non-transient messages, universal meaning, and concrete presentation provided by the use of other visual tools and aids. An effective communication system can contain elements of both systems.

What is the typical classroom (or communication environment) like?

In the average classroom, the majority of communication between teachers and students is verbal. Home and community experiences are no different. We know that many of these students perform better visually than auditorily, yet they live and learn in environments where the primary mode of communication challenges their weaker skills a majority of the time.

Since classrooms are primarily auditory, how do these students respond?

It is not uncommon for teachers and caregivers of students with autism and those experiencing communication disorders or behavior problems to make observations about the student's style of participation. Common descriptions include:

> *"He is really inconsistent."*

> *"She just does what she wants."*

> *"He manipulates everyone."*

> *"She doesn't pay attention."*

> *"He 'tunes out' all the time."*

> *"He is so rigid that he follows the routine, even when things change."*

> *"She can't handle change."*

> *"He really has behavior problems when we do something new."*

These same observers are apt to describe the student's ability to listen:

"He understands everything I say but he is just being bad."

"He knows exactly what I want."

"He understands me. He is just being stubborn. He'll do it when he wants to."

Even inconsistent student performance and participation convinces teachers that the student understands. Lack of compliance with directions is then interpreted as a behavior that the student is choosing.

Careful observation of these students reveals many of them experience significant difficulty effectively using the auditory information around them. The problem is not hearing acuity, but the process of attending to, receiving, processing, and making meaning from what is heard and then acting upon that information. As we critically watch these students function, we realize that they rely heavily on gestural and other visual cues and established routines in their environment for information. Their comprehension of the demands in their environment is based more on piecing together environmental visual information and expected routines rather than understanding specific verbal messages. [4]

> As educators, those of us who are students of "language" may have been trained in the strategies of "language stimulation" and "language expansion". Functionally, that can translate into "talking a lot". The less the child does, the more we talk. Observation of real life interactions reveals lots of students are being bombarded with more language than they can hope to comprehend.

Can you give me an example?

Here is one:

Joan arrives home from school and is standing in the hallway. Mother takes her by the hand and leads her to the closet and says, "Take off your coat and put your lunch box in the kitchen." Joan follows the directions. Is Joan responding to the words or performing a routine when given a cue to begin?

Here's another example:

Mark begins to help clean off the table after lunch. When he picks up a cup, the teacher tells him to put it in the sink while pointing to the sink. Mark puts it in the sink. What cues is he responding to? Is he receiving more information from the teacher's speech or the objects and gestures he sees?

What about this situation:

The teacher hands Mary an empty milk carton and tells her to put it on the teacher's desk. Mary carries the empty carton to the waste basket and throws it away. What cues have meaning for Mary? She responded with a learned routine that she associated with that carton.

Does that mean we should teach students not to follow those cues?

Is it bad that these students are attending to gestural and situational cues? Of course not! All communicators rely heavily on visual information to accurately interpret messages. This is how researchers describe the normal communication message. They say it is:

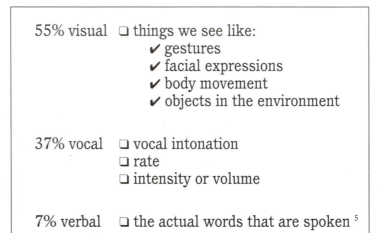

55% visual ❏ things we see like:
  ✔ gestures
  ✔ facial expressions
  ✔ body movement
  ✔ objects in the environment

37% vocal ❏ vocal intonation
  ❏ rate
  ❏ intensity or volume

7% verbal ❏ the actual words that are spoken [5]

Pay attention to students who are described like this:
- *He is just manipulative.*
- *He acts like he is deaf.*
- *She's inconsistent.*
- *He is very distractible.*
- *She's off in another world.*
- *He does just what he wants to.*
- *She doesn't pay attention.*
- *I know he understands-he just doesn't want to do it.*
- *She understands everything I say.*
- *Sometimes he clicks and sometimes he doesn't.*
- *She doesn't like to listen.*
- *She is being stubborn.*
- *He can do other things so he should be able to do this.*

If we have established that our targeted students understand auditory information even less than normal listeners, consider what a small part verbal language may actually be in their comprehension of communication.

Lack of cooperation or lack of independence may really be the result of those students not understanding fully what is expected of them or what is going to happen. *They may be accurately interpreting only fragments of the communication message.* It is helpful to observe if students with communication disorders can utilize and make sense of supporting information. It is also helpful to have a sense of how much of the verbal part of the message they comprehend. Understanding which cues have the most impact on a student's comprehension will significantly affect programming and training goals.

How can I use this information? What should I think about so I will meet the needs of these students?

CONSIDER THIS:

Think of these students as 90% visual and 10% auditory. These numbers are not based on significant statistical evidence, but rather, on observation. The numbers serve only to establish a mind set...an attitude. How would you communicate with them if they were 90% visual and 10% auditory? How would you educate them? Many students function that way even if their hearing acuity is normal.

> *How would you educate someone who was 90% visual and 10% auditory?*

Does that mean that changing my program will give my students communication skills that are age appropriate?

As professionals working with students with special needs, we would like to remediate or eliminate their areas of difficulty. Frequently, we are not in the business of "fixing" or "curing" kids. There is a part of disability or an identified learning style that may always be there. The goal of education will be maximizing the student's individual ability. Toward that end, three goals are appropriate and realistic.

1. Teach Skills

We need to help students maximize the skill potential they do have. They need to learn strategies to make their communication interactions as *effective*, as *efficient*, as *universal*, and *socially acceptable* as possible.

2. Teach Compensatory Strategies

Students who learn to use visual supports to help them accomplish their goals will benefit from increased participation and greater independence. That independence is certainly a long term educational goal.

3. Modify Environments for Maximum Learning

Utilize the knowledge we have about how these students learn. Modifying environments and creating teaching strategies so they have an opportunity to learn more efficiently will maximize their learning time.

The typical environment relies on verbalization as the primary mode of communication. Communication can become more efficient for some students by capitalizing on their visual strengths.

At the risk of sounding like a "magic cure" it is safe to state that almost all students can benefit from some forms of visual tools used as a part of their communication systems.

These thoughts suggest some rethinking about the programming goals for my students.

Be encouraged to look at your students and their learning environments through the "eye of communication." Consider both receptive and expressive elements when evaluating communication participation. Consider the use of visual supports as an option when needed to mediate communication or create environmental supports. The implementation of visual supports will be one of the pieces of a comprehensive communication system.

There is a lot to think about. Where do I begin?

Let's start surveying samples of visual tools and exploring how they are used.

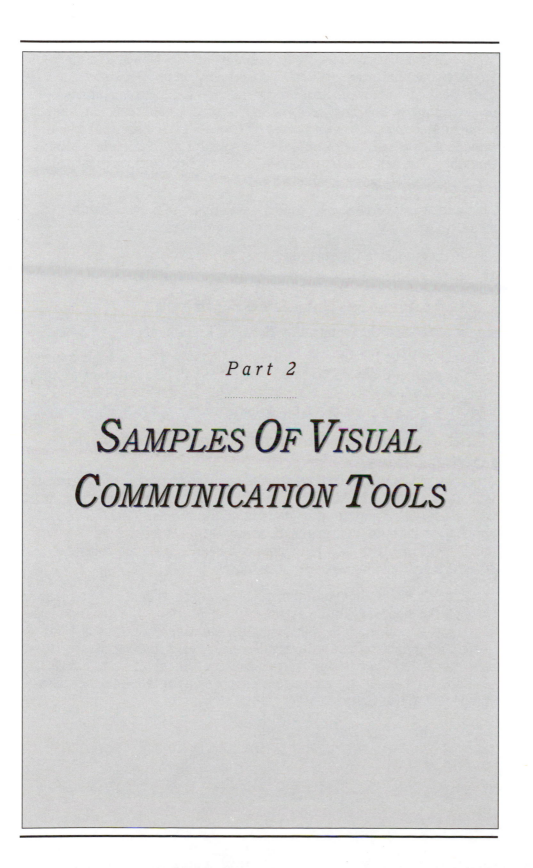

Part 2

SAMPLES OF VISUAL COMMUNICATION TOOLS

Visual tools are created for a purpose: they are developed as a means to support communication. When a communication problem exists, a consistent communication breakdown occurs, an environment needs to be organized, or behavior needs to be modified, visual tools can be implemented to assist the process. The intent of this section is to provide a wide variety of samples in various forms to stimulate your thinking. The samples have been selected to demonstrate their use across a span of ages and ability levels.

This part will be organized into four sections to help describe the visual options:

■ Tools to Give Information

■ Aids to Give Effective Directions

■ Visual Strategies to Organize the Environment

■ Mediating Communication Between Environments

Examples will be included to demonstrate how to develop tools to meet specific needs. It should be noted that there will be some natural overlap between sections. Many of the tools suggested can be developed to serve more than one function.

What student age and ability level is appropriate for these tools?

Any idea can be customized to provide support at a level appropriate for individual needs. The ideas presented here have been adapted to work with students ranging from toddlers to adults. These strategies have application for students ranging in ability from severe mental impairment to gifted. Most students will benefit from the concrete structure provided by many of these tools.

It is recommended that you think of some target students as you browse through the samples. In the beginning, consider how the general ideas would have application to your student's situations. The specific format needed for individual use will vary depending on a number of considerations. Part IV will discuss more specifically how to assess your students, analyze your environment, and plan the details of tools you decide to use.

Chapter 2

Tools To Give Information

A major function of communication is to give information. In the typical school or home environment:

- a majority of the information is given verbally

- it is frequently *assumed* that the students already know or remember specific information

- the assumption that students already know results in information not being given at all.

Visual aids such as schedules and calendars are tools whose primary function is to give information in a logical, structured, sequential form. Most people use some of these types of supports to organize their own daily lives. Our targeted students benefit from their use, too. Since these tools in traditional forms may not give enough information for some students, adaptations and enhancements increase the amount of information available, to make them more meaningful.

Giving information to students in a concrete visual form helps them handle the many happenings during a day that can cause confusion or frustration. It gives them the structure necessary to better handle those situations that are difficult for them.

Presenting information in a visual form:

- helps establish and maintain attention
- gives information in a form that the student can quickly and easily interpret
- clarifies verbal information
- provides a concrete way to teach concepts such as time, sequence, cause/effect
- gives the structure to understand and accept change
- supports transitions between activities or locations

SCHEDULES

Imagine being on one of those whirlwind package tours of Europe; sixteen cities in 7 days. You discover the tour agent forgot to give you an itinerary. Every day you don't know where you are going, what you are going to see or when you are going to eat. Frustrating? That is how many of our students feel about life on a daily basis. It is one of the reasons we see students cling to ritual and routine.

Using scheduling devices provides one of the greatest returns for your effort when setting up a smoothly running classroom. There are so many benefits in improved student understanding and cooperation. The schedules help the classroom become more organized, which helps students perform more consistently.

But my students know our routine. Is a schedule really necessary?

It is easy to assume students know their schedules and routines. In reality they frequently don't, or they don't remember, or they forget, or are not sure, or they don't want to do what they are supposed to be doing, or they get distracted, etc.,etc. Schedules help clarify communication between staff and students. They are useful for redirecting students back to the activity of the moment. In addition, the schedule can be the foundation point for many of the other communication tools used in the environment.

Daily Schedule: **Tuesday**		
🕐 8:00	Circle Time	
🕐 8:30	Play Time	
🕐 9:00	Story Time	
🕐 9:30	Snack	
🕐 10:00	Outdoor Play	
🕐 10:30	Music	
🕐 11:00	Learning Centers	

The schedule gives the student information such as:

- what is happening today (regular activities)
- what is happening today(something new, different, unusual)
- what is not happening today
- what is the sequence of events
- what is changing that I normally expect
- when it is time to stop one activity and move on to another one

SAMPLES & EXAMPLES

PROBLEM: Chris climbs off the bus at 8:00 in the morning. He longingly eyes the lunch box he is carrying and announces he wants lunch. When the teacher tells him he has to wait until lunch time to eat it, he initiates a long temper tantrum.

SOLUTION: A verbal retort like "You can't eat now. You have to wait until lunch time," won't pacify Chris. When is that? To help him understand, develop a daily schedule to guide him through the sequence of events that lead up to lunch. Then, when he wants his lunch in the morning, you can refer to the schedule to show him what activities need to occur before lunch. The schedule will help establish a routine to be followed that is clear to Chris.

PROBLEM: Karl knows that he goes to gym every day after lunch. On days that the gym teacher is absent, Karl has a tantrum because the routine is changed and he doesn't get to go.

SOLUTION: Create Karl's daily schedule with gym in it. Then visually show him there is a change by crossing out or covering up gym and showing the alternate activity. Let Karl participate in the changing of the item in the schedule to help him understand it.

PROBLEM: Sarah has difficulty doing the same activities as the rest of the class. When it is time for one activity to stop and another one to start, she is apt to resist the change. Instead of staying with the group during an activity, she wanders around the room or runs to the play area to pull out toys.

SOLUTION: Use the schedule to engage Sarah in establishing a routine for changing activities. When it is time to change, go to the schedule to remove the last activity and identify what comes next. Use the schedule to redirect Sarah back to the current activity if she leaves it. Show her and tell her, "the schedule says_____."

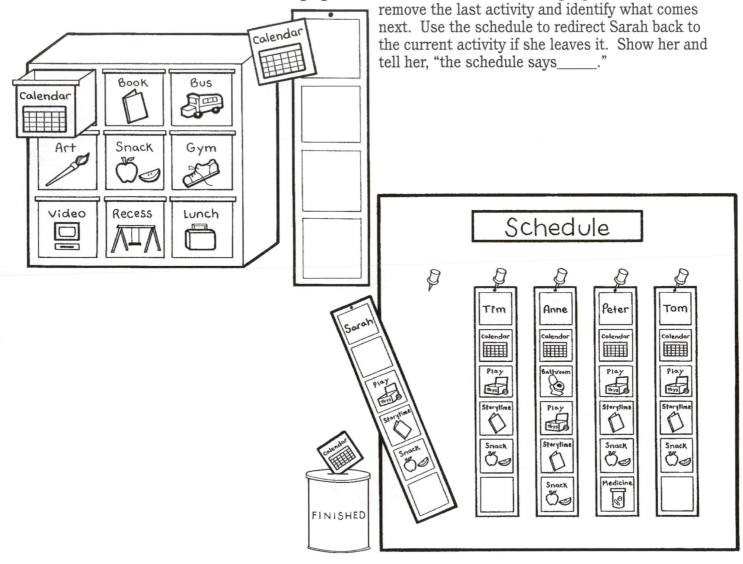

HOW TO CREATE A DAILY SCHEDULE

1. DIVIDE THE DAY INTO SEGMENTS

Identify segments that are noticeably different to the student. For example, note:

- changes from one room to another

- changes in location within the classroom (from the big table to individual desks or from sitting on carpet squares in one corner to a circle of chairs across the room)

- changes in activity that use different materials

- changes in staff

It is not necessary or possible to list every single activity in a day. That would make the schedule too cumbersome. Select the major activities; what is most noticeable or meaningful to the student. How much you include will depend on what your students will understand. Remember, mini-schedules can be developed to detail specific time slots or individual activities. (see Mini-Schedules, page 39)

2. GIVE EACH SEGMENT A NAME

Make sure the names of the segments convey some idea about the location or overall activity from the student's perspective. Try names like:

Schedule Time	*O.T.*	*Music*
Jobs	*Work Time*	*Cooking*
Lunch	*Make Lunch*	*Clean Up*
Math Corner	*Bathroom*	*Circle Time*
Aerobics	*Video Games*	*Group Time*
Independent Work Time	*Gym*	*Leisure*
Break	*Game Time*	*Library*
Shopping	*Seat Work*	*Art Table*
Computer Lab	*Room 16*	*Music*
Today At School	*Mrs. Sohn's Room*	*Training Trip*

Some activity names are very specific (Aerobics). Others can be more generic (Work Time) where different activities may be included in that time slot on different days.

It is surprising how many classrooms glide from one activity to another without giving students specific names for what is occurring. Think about what things you do that you do not give a name, or that are called different names at different times.

Special needs for individual students can be added to the main schedule or to their individual schedules:

Take Your Pills   *Bathroom*   *O.T.*

3.SELECT A REPRESENTATION SYSTEM

Pick a form that is easily recognized by your students. You want them to be able to identify the items quickly and consistently. Students will benefit more from scheduling activities if recognizing the symbols is as effortless as possible. When creating a schedule for the whole class, choose a form that will be easily interpreted by all the students. It is better to use a simpler format that everyone can understand, rather than make it more complex and miss connecting with part of the group.

Consider using:

- written words

- pictographs, line drawings

- photographs

- signs, logos, objects

Combinations of words and some form of graphics is frequently the best choice. When using pictures, label them with the exact words you will use to refer to the activity. Many pictures that come from picture books or language programs are already labeled for different purposes. Change the words on the pictures to accurately represent what you say when you communicate with that picture. Labeling the items increases their effectiveness because:

- everyone will use consistent terminology when referring to activities. The combined system results in more rapid recognition for most students.

- many students will learn to read the words that accompany the pictures.

4. SELECT A FORMAT

Who is it for:
- group schedule
- individual schedule
- both

How will it get a perspective of time:
- does it need specific times to coordinate with bells and school functions
- is sequence of activities more important than specific times for student understanding
- some of each

What will it look like:
- wall chart
- photocopied and passed out
- in a book, folder, or 3-ring binder
- in plastic strips or pages
- written on paper to fold for a pocket
- to fit in a wallet
- hang on a clipboard
- written on the blackboard

How big does it need to be:
- big enough to see from across the room
- small enough to fit in a pocket
- maneuverable enough for small hands
- "normal" enough so it doesn't attract unusual attention
- portable enough to meet individual mobility needs

Where will it be located:
- hang on a wall
- place on desk or table
- carry in a pocket
- carry in personal folder or binder or book
- other

How mobile does it need to be:
- students stay in one classroom most of the time
- students move to several locations

5. DECIDE HOW THE STUDENTS WILL PARTICIPATE IN SCHEDULE PREPARATION AT THE BEGINNING OF THE DAY

The students should begin each day with some form of activity giving them the opportunity to create and discuss their daily schedule. Participating in the assembly of the schedule is important. Students iternalize the information better if they actively participate, rather than just looking at something prepared by another person.

What will the activity be:
- teacher writes or assembles schedule for the class
- student watches and discusses with teacher
- student copies schedule with pencil & paper, typewriter, computer
- student assembles own picture schedule in holders, copying master schedule
- student photocopies teacher schedule

How will schedule preparation be handled:
- an individual activity
- a group activity

REMEMBER: Having the student participate in the assembly of the schedule in some way is a critical part in helping him orient to the activities of the day. The way this activity is handled will depend on student age and ability to understand, but active participation is one of the most valuable elements of using a schedule system.

6. DECIDE HOW THE SCHEDULE WILL BE USED THROUGHOUT THE DAY

The teacher or the student indicates when the activity is over by referring back to the schedule.

Develop an activity routine:
Follow some routine motor action to acknowledge the transition.

- cross off or check off what was completed
- turn the picture over
- take the completed item off the chart
- identify next activity

- point to new activity and use a verbal routine
- move to new activity
- carry schedule picture or object or other visible cue to guide transition to new location if necessary

Develop a verbal routine:
Make the process of using and changing the schedule a language activity. Either the teacher or the student should talk through the change of activity.

Use a verbal script to accompany the motor routines (suggested above). "Leisure time is finished. Time for Work Stations." This procedure helps students attend to the transition. It teaches them an organized routine that they will be able to follow to handle situations more independently.

Encourage students to actively participate in the verbal routine. Even nonverbal or limited verbal students should be a part of this. Try using a fill-in-the-blank type activity. "Leisure time is finished. Time for_____." Make sure students take their turn to fill in the blank with whatever means they have. Their turn might be removing the picture, a gesture or a vocalization. What is important is to produce something when it is their turn. Many students have acquired a significant functional vocabulary from the repetitive use of the verbal scripts in this activity.

Students who have more language will engage in communication beyond the simple script. Talk about what is finished and what comes next. This is a good time to discuss:

- what will happen

- where to go

- what material will be needed

- what rules to follow

> *The most artistic, beautiful, wonderful schedule will not achieve its potential unless it is used as an integral part of the daily program.*

7. HOW TO USE THE SCHEDULE
- follow it
- if you are not going to follow it-change it
- make it an essential part of the daily routine
- continually refer back to it when communicating about its information
- treat it as a valuable tool
- allow enough time in your plans to use it effectively
- allow it to guide the structure of your environment
- use it as a source to stimulate conversation and language enrichment

REMEMBER: Integrating the schedule into the flow of daily activity will maximize its value.

8. USE THE SCHEDULE TO COMMUNICATE WITH OTHERS
The daily schedule is a terrific resource to help students improve their ability to communicate about their lives to other people. The schedule can serve as a tool to support communicating information to people in different environments.

- use the schedule as a tool to support communication with others
- take home the schedule or a copy of the schedule
- use the schedule to help create a form of home-school communication

Mediating Communication Between Environments (Chapter 5) will elaborate on ways to use schedule information to enhance communication opportunities.

MINI-SCHEDULES

The daily schedule helps to guide the students through the major segments and transitions of his day. It is too cumbersome to include every activity and movement in that main daily schedule. **MINI-SCHEDULES** are practical and convenient systems to supplement the daily schedule. The mini-schedule directs the choices or sequence of activities during a shorter time segment or a particular activity period.

Example: The daily schedule indicates it is time for COOKING. The student goes to his mini-schedule to find that during food preparation time he is going to 1)make a sandwich, 2)make ice tea, and 3)set the table.

Mini-schedules can be in the same format as the daily schedule but they do not need to be. Since the mini-schedule is used to guide a smaller portion of the day, it is possible to include considerably more detail as necessary to accomplish the goals.

Isn't it going to be confusing having all those schedules floating around?

Not if they are well coordinated. An effective system of organization is to label the mini-schedule with the same symbol that is represented on the daily schedule. Then the student learns to identify the activity on the main schedule and look for the mini schedule that has that same symbol. There is an obvious relationship between the two. It will be important to have a storage location to keep tools so they can be accessed easily when needed.

What do the mini-schedules accomplish?

There are two main purposes.

1. Like the daily schedules, they give the student information about the activities that will be occurring.

2. The mini-schedules provide an excellent structure to teach independent work habits. As students master the ability to transition from one activity to another by following the schedule, that procedure can be expanded to teach them to work for longer periods of time with less supervision.

SAMPLES & EXAMPLES

go to your
locker

hang your
coat

hang your
backpack

put your notebook
in the basket

PROBLEM: Jake demonstrates a variety of behavior problems when going through the transition of getting off the school bus and into his classroom. He frequently won't carry his school bag, sits down on the sidewalk or attempts to run away from staff. Since he hasn't even gotten into the school building he hasn't had an opportunity to put together his daily schedule to give him some structure.

SOLUTION: Create a mini-schedule that contains the steps necessary to get from the bus to the classroom. It seemed that Jake got so carried away by his behaviors and manipulations during the transition process that he forgot what he was actually supposed to be doing. By showing and telling Jake what the next step was, it helped him ignore the distractions and focus on what his next purposeful action should be. The staff had Jake carry the mini-schedule and referred to it frequently, reiterating what they were doing as they were performing each step of the sequence.

PROBLEM: Paul has trouble staying on task to follow the classroom routines. When he needs to accomplish a sequence of steps to manage a routine, he gets distracted by the air conditioner, the computer, and other objects in the environment. Regular routines such as coming into school in the morning are frustrating because Paul needs a lot more direction and redirection than the other students.

SOLUTION: Develop mini-schedules to guide Paul through his daily routines to develop more independence.

Schedule and Mini-schedule Format

MAIN SCHEDULE		Paul's MINI-SCHEDULE	Mary's MINI-SCHEDULE
8:30	arrival	coat lunch box notes to teacher bathroom play	
8:45	greetings		
9:00	academics	make shopping list work on computer bathroom	make shopping list cut coupons get money ready
9:30	snack	set table	make juice put away food clean up
10:00	shopping		
11:00	cooking	make French toast	set table get out condiments prepare dessert
11:30	lunch		
12:15	grooming	take medication bathroom brush teeth wash face comb hair	

The main schedule lists the general activity for each time slot through the day. The mini-schedules lead students through individual sequences of activities within each time slot. There are two types of mini-schedules:

1. Supports to perform regular, unchanging routines

2. Guides to give information for time slots where the specific activity may change on a daily or regular basis

Mini-schedules are used only if a student needs them. For example, during arrival and grooming times, Paul needs the scheduling prompts to follow the regular routine. Mary is able to perform those recurring routines without the extra support. Both students have mini-schedules for the time slots that have changing activities. Those mini-schedules are changed on a daily basis to accommodate for the daily lesson plan.

PROBLEM: The teacher would like the students to learn to work more independently for longer periods of time. She would like them to be able to begin a job, complete it, and transition to the next job without teacher prompting.

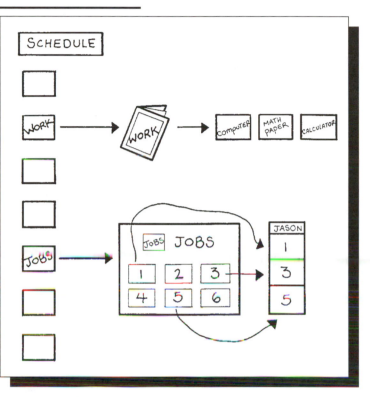

SOLUTION: Develop some mini-schedules to guide the students through a series of activities to work independently.

The daily schedule lists the main activity segments. Each student has a mini-schedule holder labeled with the same wording and symbol that is on the schedule for that time. The teacher or student prepares the mini-schedule, which contains the individual activities to be accomplished during that time slot.

There is a time for ROOM JOBS in the daily schedule. In the morning, when the students are assembling their schedules, they go to the ROOM JOBS board to select specific ROOM JOBS that they insert into a holder. Then, when they reach that point in the day, they go to their ROOM JOBS mini-schedule to recall which activities they chose for that time period. The students then follow that mini-schedule to accomplish the sequence of jobs selected.

HOW TO DEVELOP A MINI-SCHEDULE

Creating a mini-schedule will follow the same general procedure as producing a daily schedule. It is important to remember that mini-schedules do not have to replicate the form and format of the daily schedule. For example: The classroom schedule might be done in black and white drawings, but the mini-schedules are created in photographs or written lists or whatever form seems most appropriate considering the individual student and what specific items are being included. Perhaps the class schedule hangs on a bulletin board or is carried in the student's pocket, but the mini-schedule is in a small picture book or hangs in a work area.

REMEMBER: Developing a daily schedule is generally geared toward managing a whole class. The format should be as generic as possible to meet the broadest needs. Mini-schedules offer more individualization during targeted time slots. The format for these can be designed to target more specific individual learning goals.

Being able to predict or anticipate the activities of the day gives students a sense of control, security, and independence

When students have difficulty stopping activities or transitioning to less preferred activities, the teacher can "blame" the schedule. "The Schedule says it is time for___"

THE POINT IS: Schedules can:

- give students information about their lives

- help students see a logic and order to their world

- serve as a communication aid to discuss and share daily events

- improve vocabulary and language skills

- assist in developing time concepts

- teach sequence, before and after

- reduce or eliminate behavior problems related to transitions and changing activities

REMEMBER: The schedule can be the anchor and foundation for many of the other communication tools in a well organized program. The pictures and/or words in the schedule are used for labels to organize locations, activities or other communication tools. The following chapters will give more examples of how that will work.

CALENDARS

CALENDARS are a common tool in classrooms. The way they are used, however, varies significantly in different environments. Traditional calendar activities such as reciting day and date and memorizing days of the week and months of the year may have little functional value for many students, particularly those with more severe disabilities. There are other less common ways that calendars can support students.

Forget the recitation activities! I depend on my personal calendar for survival. I have one I carry in my purse. I'd be lost without it. I never thought about my students benefiting in the same way I do.

Yes! Calendars can be just as valuable for our students. They successfully help students organize their lives, understand sequence and time concepts, and give them much valuable information. Think about all the things students ask about and would like to know that can be put on a calendar. Calendars are used to tell students:

- which days are school days / not school days
- when regular special events or activities will occur
- when irregular activities will occur
- field trips/training trips
- when someone is coming / going
- how long someone will be here / gone
- appointments such as doctor, hair cut
- who will be at home after school
- when a baby-sitter will be coming
- which days student will be leaving school early or coming to school late
- the lunch menu / when to bring & when to buy
- when to bring things to school or take things home
- when to bring money / how much to bring

HERE'S WHAT TO DO:
Develop a classroom calendar
Teach students to go to the calendar to get information. Part of the daily schedule time can be devoted to looking at the calendar to review what is going to be happening.

Develop a calendar at home
Most families have a calendar hanging somewhere. Even though the calendar is there, the targeted student may not know how to use it. It may not be used with the intent of giving him specific information about his life. An effective home calendar can give information about each family member in a way that our students will be able to understand. Get him his own calendar. Don't try to put everything on it; just those things that are important to him.

Develop the use of personal calendars or daily planners
Create individual calendars to include personal information for the student's life. To increase personal responsibility and independence, teach students to develop their own calendars to organize their lives. Teach them how to write in information to help remember what they are responsible for. Teach them a routine for checking their calendars to access information. The current trend in the business world is to carry a daily planner of some kind. Teach your students that system.

day	Thursday	Friday	Saturday
X	3 Swim	4 X	5 X
	10 Swim	11	12
	17 Swim	18	19
	24 Swim	25	26

SAMPLES & EXAMPLES

PROBLEM: Sam loves to swim so much that his mother takes him to the community pool every Thursday,. Beginning Friday, he asks her many times a day the equivalent of , "Are we going swimming today?" A verbal response to his request was unsuccessful in reducing the perseverative questioning.

SOLUTION: Use a calendar to give Sam information. Mom hung a calendar on the refrigerator. On every Thursday she put a picture to represent swimming. Mom taught Sam how to make an X at the end of each day and then look to see how many more days until swimming. Once the calendar was on the refrigerator, Mom used it to answer Sam's question. When he asked, she took him to the calendar to show him today. She told him "No swimming" when showing him where to look. On Wednesday she told him, "We go swimming tomorrow." On Thursday she talked with him about swimming today. Every time Sam asked about swimming Mom referred him to the calendar. After a short while, Mom observed that Sam was going to the calendar independently to look many times a day. Simultaneously, his questioning reduced significantly. The calendar gave him the information he wanted.

On Thursday, Sam's questioning skyrocketed. He knew it was swimming day, but didn't understand when. Mom used a picture to represent dinner to show him that swimming was after dinner. She mounted a dinner picture and a swimming picture on the refrigerator right next to the calendar and used the pair of pictures to answer his questions. Again, once Sam understood the meaning of the pictures, he began to use them to answer his own questions.

PROBLEM: Sam has difficulty handling changes in his schedule. If he expects a particular routine and that routine is changed, Mom can expect to encounter a significant behavior problem in protest. Swimming was canceled one week. Mom wanted to avoid a predictable problem.

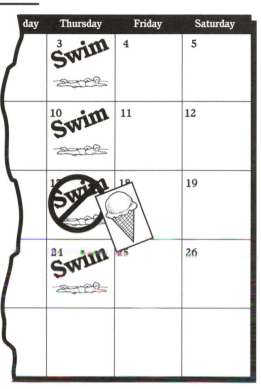

SOLUTION: To help Sam understand, Mom put a "NO" sign on the swimming picture to show Sam that something was different. Mom then decided to plan an alternate activity so Sam would still have an outing that day. A picture of an ice cream cone was added to the calendar next to the "NO swimming" so Mom could tell Sam about the schedule change. As Sam became accustomed to using the calendar, Mom was able to add more significant scheduling information to help reduce Sam's perseverative questioning and help him handle changes.

PROBLEM: Tim has great difficulty remembering what he needs to bring to school and when. Because of his schedule, he brings his lunch some days, eats in the cafeteria some days, and brings money to shop for supplies to cook his own lunch on other days. Parents and teacher have been trying unsuccessfully to get him to assume more responsibility with remembering but Tim's success has been minimal.

SOLUTION: The teacher sits down with Tim on Friday and discusses the activities for the coming week. Tim writes on his calendar what the specific needs are for each day and takes it home. Mom is teaching Tim to look at the calendar each evening as part of his "getting ready for tomorrow" routine. Then Tim has the responsibility for packing his lunch or getting the money ready for the next day.

Sunday	Monday	Tuesday	Wednesday	Thursday	Friday	Saturday
		1	2	3	4	5
6	7 Pack Lunch	8 Hot Lunch $1.50	9 Grocery Shopping $2.00	10 Pack Lunch	11 McDonalds $3.00	12

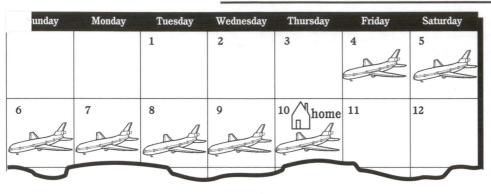

unday	Monday	Tuesday	Wednesday	Thursday	Friday	Saturday
		1	2	3	4 ✈	5 ✈
6 ✈	7 ✈	8 ✈	9 ✈	10 🏠 home	11	12

PROBLEM: Jerry's parents will be going away for a one week vacation. During that time he will be staying with a sitter. Jerry's parents are concerned that he will not understand they will be coming back.

SOLUTION: Jerry's parents created a calendar that told Jerry how many days they would be gone. Since they were going away on an airplane, they told Jerry what they were doing and used the airplane symbol to indicate that they were gone. They placed a different picture to show the day they would return home. Jerry's babysitters could use the calendar to show Jerry that his parents were still gone and how many days remained before they returned.

unday	Monday	Tuesday	Wednesday	Thursday	Friday	Saturday
		1	2	3	4	5 Jenny's house 🎂
6	7	8	9	10	11	12
13	14	15 Jenny's house 🎂	16 Jenny's house 🎂	17 Jenny's house 🎂	18 Jenny's house 🎂	19

PROBLEM: Scott's parents faced a similar situation: going away and leaving Scott for a longer than usual time. Since Scott had flown on an airplane they suspected that he would become upset if he knew that they were going and he was not.

SOLUTION: They decided to use a calendar but to focus the symbols on what Scott was doing instead of on the parent's activity. They told Scott that he was going to "Jenny's house with the swimming pool." Since Scott went to Jenny's for an occasional weekend, they began to use the symbols with him whenever he went there so he would be comfortable using them by the time the longer trip came.

THE POINT IS: Calenders can:

- give students information in a form that they understand

- be a tool to mediate communication about daily, weekly and monthly events

- answer student questions

- teach strategies to become more independent

- give students some organizational strategies to manage themselves

- help students see a logic and order to life; teach sequence, before and after

- reduce or eliminate behavior problems for students who resist change or experience difficulty when they don't understand what is happening

REMEMBER: Calendars can be used by students with a wide range of abilities. A student does not need to be able to speak or read to use the calendar concept successfully. Knowing or reciting days of the week or months of the year are not prerequisites and are actually unnecessary skills for meaningful calendar use.

CHOICE BOARDS AND MENUS

One of the simplest and most commonly used communication tools, the **CHOICE BOARD** is frequently devised to introduce students to the use of visual communication. Choosing a food selection from several choices provides immediate reinforcement and is an effective way to teach pointing and requesting, even for students who display little communicative intent. Making choices is frequently one of the first functions taught to more severely handicapped students.

I use choice boards with my students at snack time. Is there more that I can do with them?

The concept of the choice board is broadened considerably when you think of it as a menu to give students information. Menus work great for non-food selections and other activities besides eating. Consider menus or choices for things such as:

■ leisure activities

■ who to work or play with

■ which restaurant to go to

■ which store to go to

■ which job do you want to do

■ which song to sing

■ which game or activity to do

■ who gets a turn

■ which work area to go to

■ places to visit

■ what to eat for snack or meal

■ to participate or not participate in an activity

The menu tells what the selections are and gives an opportunity to scan the options before making a decision.

REMEMBER: The choice selection can be represented in some printed form, but it is frequently convenient to use the actual objects to present choices. Whichever method is used, enabling the student to see the choices tends to be a better option than just a verbal request.

That is a nice idea, but shouldn't I be making those choices for my students? I am the one in charge. It's not good discipline to let them "run the show".
Giving students the opportunity to make choices is a way of giving them more control over their lives. Having some opportunity for self-determination will increase their level of participation. Giving choices does not mean that a student insurrection will take place. You are still in charge. You control the options. There are times when the student has a choice and there are times when he does not.

But all the choices are not available all the time. How do you handle that?
Menus tell students when an item is available. More importantly, they can tell students when a choice is not available. This is particularly helpful for the students who persist with a request that will not be available for some reason. Visual tools such as a "NO" sign, a schedule or a calendar can help clarify this type of situation. Let's look at some ways this can work.

SAMPLES & EXAMPLES

PROBLEM: During snack time the teacher opens Jackie's lunch box, selects one of the items and gives it to Jackie. Jackie throws it.

WHY: Jackie really wanted a different food item from the lunch box, and that was his way of protesting.

SOLUTION: Give him an opportunity to make a choice from viewing the options from the lunch box. (In addition, Jackie needs to learn to communicate his protest in a more acceptable manner.)

Leisure

ping pong

video games

magazines

cards

roller blades

PROBLEM: When given free time, Sherrie selects the same activity all the time.

WHY: She likes that activity. She may not remember what other choices she has. She has established a routine that is difficult to change.

SOLUTION: Provide a menu of activities for Sherrie to choose from. Some people would suggest not putting Sherrie's favorite activity on the menu since they don't want her to spend her time doing it. Another strategy may be more effective. Include it. When Sherrie chooses it, let her do it for a short while. Then, make a change. Have her cover up that item on the menu and make another selection. Repeat this procedure so Sherrie can sample several of the choices. If Sherrie tries to choose her favored activity again, show her that it is "all done".

PROBLEM: Steve requests the opportunity to watch a video. It is not something he can choose now.

WHY: Either it is all done, or not available, or the teacher does not want it to be a choice.

SOLUTION: Cover the item on the menu or use a "NO" sign to indicated that it is not available. There is a tendency for people to handle this type of situation by removing that option from the menu. The problem is, even if the item is not on the menu, Steve remembers it. He will keep requesting it and requesting it. By leaving the item on the menu, the teacher can use the menu as a tool to communicate its unavailability. Covering it up or using the "NO" sign is a way of giving Steve more information. He may not like the answer, but at least he understands the communication about the situation. If this is a persistent problem and video is available only on specific days, introduce a calendar to show Steve when it is a choice.

REMEMBER: Some people remove a symbol from the communication tool when they don't want a student to request it. This causes problems when the student remembers the item and wants to request it. Without the symbol present it is more difficult to communicate about it. When the item or symbol of the item is still available, the teacher can acknowledge the request by calling attention to the fact it is not available and urge the student to make another choice. This strategy provides for more effective communication.

THE POINT IS: Choice boards and menus:

- give the opportunity to teach acceptable requesting behavior
- broaden the range of possible choices a student can have
- help him make a greater variety of selections
- improve communication effectiveness
- provide a reliable way to indicate something is not available
- reduce idiosyncratic requesting and protesting behavior

COMMUNICATING "NO"

When giving students information, it is just as important to be able to let them know what is not available or what is not an option as it is to give them choices. It is frequently helpful to clarify communication by telling students:

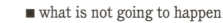

- what is not a choice
- what is not acceptable behavior
- what is not going to happen

Deciding what the options should be on choice boards or menus can be a challenge. It is not uncommon for the teacher to think of several options that the teacher wants, only to find out that what the student really wants is not one of those choices. The student's desired choices may be something the teacher does not want to be an option for some reason. Clarifying this in a visual form supports mutual understanding.

Similarly, it is important to be able to communicate clearly what behavior is *not* acceptable, what you don't want the student to do, or what event is *not* going to happen. Visual strategies communicate these concepts in a concrete manner.

Isn't it better to tell things in a positive way instead of negative: telling them what is going to happen or what positive behavior you want from them?

Although it is considered most desirable to present information to students in a positive manner, there are times when giving the negative side is equally helpful. Tools can contain both positive and negative information to clarify communication.

This sounds like a good idea. How do you do it?

The international NO (⊘) sign has proven helpful to visually represent the concept. Positioned next to or on top of a picture or used by itself, it is easily recognized even by students who display limited recognition of printed material. Other ways to indicate NO include turning items over, covering them up, crossing them out, or removing them from the set of choices. Consider these situations:

SAMPLES & EXAMPLES

PROBLEM: The teacher keeps some of her supplies in a cupboard that she doesn't want the students to open. Tommy keeps wandering over to that cupboard to take a look. He takes things out and carries them around the room.

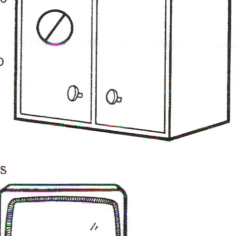

SOLUTION: Put a NO sign on the cupboard to remind Tommy not to go in it . When he goes to the cupboard, show him the sign and remind him what it says.

PROBLEM: Vince has targeted the family VCR as an enticing toy. When he is in the room where it is located, he constantly leaves his toys to go push the buttons on the machine. Even if his parents redirect him to go play with the toys, it is only a short time until he returns to play with the buttons.

SOLUTION: Put a sign on the VCR that says "NO TOUCHING". Every time Vince goes to the VCR, show him the sign and tell him no touching. If he talks, have him repeat the rule. Then redirect him back to his toys. The goal is for the sign to remind him what the rule is. In order for this to work, it is important to teach Vince what it means.

Snacks

PROBLEM: Dale has a favorite snack. No matter how many snacks are available, he will choose a specific one. There are times, however, when the box gets empty and there is no replacement. Dale doesn't seem to understand when he is told it is all gone. He needs to learn what that means.

SOLUTION: This is a perfect opportunity to teach what that NO sign means. When the box is emptied, turn the box upside down and proclaim that it is "all gone." Have Dale participate in putting a NO sign on the box or on the picture on his snack menu. Be dramatic about going through this process. Recite a script such as, "Crackers are all gone," as you and Dale put the symbol in place. Repeat your verbal script a couple of times to reinforce what is taking place. Then guide Dale to make a different choice. It may help to keep the empty box available to repeat the process if he requests crackers again now or before you go shopping.

PROBLEM: Kevin is very rigid about the regularly scheduled events in his life. He knows that on Tuesday, Mom picks him up a little early from school to go for a doctor appointment. On one particular Tuesday the schedule changed and Mom was not coming. She told him before he left for school. But, when it was the time that she normally picks him up, Kevin began pacing the floor. He didn't remember that the plans were changed and became quite upset at the variation in his routine.

SOLUTION: Mom could have written down the change and given Kevin a paper to keep in his pocket. That's what she did when the situation occurred again. It worked. Kevin kept referring to that paper throughout the day, but it helped him handle the change in plans.

REMEMBER: Removing items may eliminate opportunities to use them for communication purposes. Leaving them visible enables them to be used to clarify the information you are attempting to communicate. Try removing the item from the list of acceptable choices, but leave it available, covered or positioned nearby, so it can still be used as a communication tool.

REMEMBER: Communicating NO in a visual form can be incorporated as part of behavior management programs or used as part of visual tools developed for other communication purposes.

THE POINT IS: Visual ways to communicate the concept of NO helps:

- clarify communication
- enhance the student's understanding
- reduce confusion
- assist the student's memory of what is not available and /or not acceptable
- reduce or avoid many behavior problems
- provide a consistent reminder to students
- reduce the amount of teacher prompting and repetition necessary

PEOPLE LOCATORS

Where is everybody? It is not unusual for students to experience insecurity or frustration from not knowing where the significant people in their lives are. When people's routines change or their comings and goings are unpredictable, that can be cause for problems. Many students experience difficulty if their routines are changed because an expected person doesn't show up. A day can be ruined if a substitute teacher is in school when the student arrives. Being uncertain about what will happen this evening at home can ruin a day. Uncertainty about tomorrow at school can ruin the evening.

I never thought about students being so affected by these situations. I guess I just thought they were being difficult or taking advantage of a situation.
Students who experience difficulty with change can be so preoccupied with people changes that their functioning is impaired. Rigidity and rituals can increase.

Giving these students more information, in a visual form, can reduce their insecurities and help them better handle the situations that come up.

PEOPLE LOCATORS give information about:

- who is here today
- who is not here
- where someone is
- who is coming later
- when someone will come
- who is supposed to come but will not
- who is not supposed to come but will

I try to remember to tell my students about those things when they come up. Isn't that enough?

It is easy to assume this information is not that significant to students. If we tell them, we think they will remember and understand. That is not necessarily so. Putting this information in visual form helps the students by giving them an opportunity to go back to it as many times as they need, to recall and reinforce what will occur. By giving students this information ahead of time, many difficulties can be averted. Let's see how it works.

SAMPLES & EXAMPLES

Sunday	Monday	Tuesday	Wednesday	Thursday	Friday	Saturday
		1	2	3	4	5
6	7 **Sue**	8 **Mom**	9 **Sue**	10 **Mom**	11 **Dad**	12
13	14 **Sue**	15 **Mom**	16 **Sue**	17 **Mom**	18 **Grandpa**	19

PROBLEM: Johnny's mother works three days a week. Some days Mom is there when he goes home from school. Other days, a babysitter or other family member greets him at the bus. Johnny asks who will be at home dozens of times a day. People tire of answering his endless questions about this. Because of his perseveration on this topic, he experiences difficulty focusing on the other activities of his school day.

SOLUTION: Make a visual tool to clarify the information. When Johnny begins to ask questions, he is encouraged to look at the tool to get the information he needs. Eventually, he has learned to look at the tool when he requires the information and his need for verbal reassurance has reduced considerably.

PROBLEM: Chris loves to go with the Physical Therapist for her Tuesday sessions. Occasionally, the PT changes her schedule due to absence or meetings or other job requirements. Chris does not handle these changes well.

SOLUTION: Develop a calendar that indicates the PT schedule. When the PT is changing her schedule, mark those changes on the calendar. Use the calendar to talk with Chris about the changes. Changing Chris' daily schedule is another technique that will give Chris information. Letting Chris know ahead of time about the changes helps.

Sunday	Monday	Tuesday	Wednesday
		1	2
6	7 **PT**	8	9
13	14 **PT**	15	16
20	21 ~~PT~~	22 →	23 **PT**
27	28 **PT**		

PROBLEM: Ralph is very aware of the comings and goings of his brother and sister. Because they are active teenagers, they are constantly in and out of the house for school, work, and social activities. Ralph expects them to come home right after school. When they don't come right away, Ralph pesters Mom repeatedly asking where they are.

SOLUTION: The family felt that it was important not to become unnecessarily accountable to Ralph. On the other hand, giving Ralph more information would make life easier for everyone. They made a refrigerator chart to give some family information about where people were and when they would be back. That chart was helpful for the whole family communicating with each other about their whereabouts. Having more information available (even if it was not always complete) comforted Ralph.

Dad	home
Mom	horse show
Chad	work
Ralph	home
Carrie	horse show

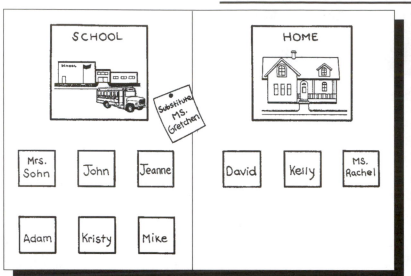

PROBLEM: In this group of students there are several reactions to other student's school attendance. Jeanne is very unaware of the presence of the other students. It is necessary to help her focus her attention to become more aware of her classmates. Adam is at the opposite extreme. He is so aware of the presence of his classmates that he asks questions about them continually if they are not in school.

SOLUTION: Develop an activity, as part of the morning routine, to identify who is at school and who is not at school (or who is at home). This activity increases the awareness of Jeanne and provides information for Adam to reduce his perseverative questioning. Include information about where the school staff are and include substitute teachers if appropriate.

THE POINT IS: People Locators are tools to:

- give students information about changes in their lives
- help students know and remember where their significant people are
- reduce anxiety
- help students accept changes in routines or expected occurrences

TRANSITION AND TRAVEL HELPERS

Stopping an activity. Starting another. Leaving one location to go across the room or to another room. The process of change can provide its own set of challenges. Although some students are unaffected by these transitions, there are many who can experience predictable difficulty during times of change. Some just don't understand what is happening. They don't figure it out. For others, resistance to change, clinging to rituals or routines, and other interrupting behaviors can create chaos in the flow of activity. Why do these problems surface? Frequently, a lack of understanding of the changes can be targeted as one piece of the puzzle. Supporting the transitions heavily with visual information is a strategy to help overcome the difficulties.

Life is full of transitions. There is no way to avoid them. What is the "magic formula" to avoid problems?

There is no magic to it, but giving information is the key. The challenge is to figure out what the student is thinking or perceiving during that time. How does the student see that situation? That will help to develop strategies to avoid problem behaviors or move the student through the transition routine.

How do I know what the student is thinking? That is not easy to figure out.

Observation of the "big picture" can frequently give some insights about what might be going on. Here are some common scripts:

- "I like what I am doing and I don't want to change."

- "I don't want to stop because I may 'never' be able to do this again."

- "I don't like to stop immediately. I need some preparation that a change is coming."

- "I need to know when I can return to this activity."

- "I don't like the upcoming activity."

- "I don't understand what is going to happen or where I am going."

- "I know what I am supposed to do, but doing it my way gets me more attention."

> *Knowing a student's tendency to be rigid, some parents and teachers will try to overcome it by creating an unstructured environment. Unfortunately, if the student is really struggling to find structure, this strategy will probably increase, rather than reduce, the student's inflexible style. Using visual supports to build in structure for the student can result in a more relaxed acceptance of what the schedule is. Then, as visual supports are used to introduce change, the student is apt to better understand what is happening. At this point he may not like what is happening, but he will handle it differently because he understands it better.*

- "I think I am doing one thing but then in the middle I find out I am doing something else and that upsets me."

- "I associate this situation with something I experienced in the past. I am afraid that something is going to happen that I didn't like at some previous time."

- "I don't want anything to change because I feel like I am losing control if it does."

- "I have a pattern of protest whenever something is different because it scares me."

- "I like routine because then I know what to expect, so anything that changes throws me in a tizzy."

Lots of times, when you ask people who know the students well to think about it, they can come up with an explanation of why the student is experiencing difficulty. People who know a student well, however, sometimes focus on the student's disruption during these transition times and fail to sit back to analyze the "big picture". Sometimes an outside observer can offer insights that those closely involved with the student fail to see.

> *Transition techniques are like a bag of tools to use when you need them. One student may need many of them on a regular basis for everything that is going on. Another student may need the support only for certain activities, only on a bad day, or only when something is new or different.*

Wow! Many of those scripts apply to the situations I deal with. Now what do I do?

Giving students information is a basis for eliminating or working through many of these difficulties. Giving that information in a visual form provides a consistency and non-transiency necessary to work through these situations. Here are several basic principles.

1. Prepare students for transitions.

Alert students that a transition is coming. Some transition times are obvious because of the natural ending of an activity (i.e., the game is finished, the job is done). Show the student with the objects and materials of the activity that an end is coming.

playing a game:	"Someone is almost at the end."
	"Someone is almost winning."
	"Just a few more spaces or a few more cards or a few more men to capture."
drying dishes:	"There are only 3 cups left and then we will be done."
dressing:	"Only one more shoe and then we will go do ____."

Other times the activity does not have a natural ending (listening to music, playing video games.) Use your visual supports or related objects to establish when a change will take place. Try these techniques:

Let student know when he begins, how long the activity will last:

- show it on the schedule
- refer to a clock or watch to indicate
- set a timer to signal how long the student has
- put a card on the student's desk that tells him he needs to stop in five minutes
- create a natural ending by establishing a certain quantity:
    - "Finish two puzzles." Put the two puzzles on the table.
    - "Listen to one side of the tape." Show him the tape.
    - "Let's sing 5 songs." Put up 5 cards to indicate 5 songs. Remove a card each time a song is done.

As the transition time approaches give the student a warning:

- refer back to the schedule- "It's almost time for____."
- refer back to a clock or watch- "Five more minutes."
- set a timer- "You have until the timer rings and then we will ___."
- create a natural ending and show it:
    - ❏ "Do three more envelopes and then we will be done: Lay out three envelopes.
    - ❏ "Only one more song and then ____." Show a picture card that represents one song.

> *Giving students information will make transitions predictable. That will help them understand their environment and reduce the potential for difficulty.*

2. Make transitions part of the routine.

Teach students to clean up or put away the materials from the previous activity and then get the materials for the new one. Those two responsibilities give them an opportunity to mentally shift.

Perceiving the transitions as a part of a familiar routine can create acceptance. Schedules and mini-schedules support the natural flow from one to another.

3. Give information and cues to prepare students for what is next.

Probably the easiest thing to do is to give students opportunities to carry things.

- carry objects
- carry the mini-schedule to the work area
- carry the supplies to the work area
- carry the shopping list to the car
- carry the towel and bathing suit on the way to swimming
- carry something to give to a person in another location

- carry pictures or cards that give information:
    - the destination when we leave the classroom
    - the destination when we leave the building
    - where we are going when we go in the car or bus
    - what we are going to get when we get to the location (i.e., ice cream)
    - what we are going to do when we get to the destination (i.e., swim)

> *It is not uncommon for parents to report the need to avoid driving past certain stores or restaurants because their child expected to stop. This rigidity can be softened by the process of giving more information.*

Some students would be more focused on *where* you are going. For other students *what will happen* is most critical. For example: When you are going out for ice cream, does the student focus on which store you are going to? Perhaps the fact that he is getting ice cream is the issue and where you purchase it is irrelevant. This is the kind of thing to think about. What is the student focusing on? Then we can give him information that will address the part that is most significant to him; the way he is thinking. Problems develop if the student thinks he is going to participate in a familiar routine and then he finds out in the middle that his expectation is not being realized.

4. Let students know when they can return to the activity they don't want to leave.

Sometimes something as simple as "You can play video games again during break time" or "Your friends can come again tomorrow" or "We will come back again next week" is enough to encourage students to change peacefully. Information like this will be more effective, however, if presented visually. Referring to break time on the daily schedule, put a picture of video games next to "break time" on the schedule. Use a calendar to indicate what will happen tomorrow or in the future. Making your information concrete will be much more meaningful than verbal information by itself.

5. If you are transitioning to an undesirable or less desirable activity, let the student know what will be happening after this thing he doesn't like.

Planning a desirable activity after an undesirable one can "up the ante" for cooperation. We all have things we don't like, but that doesn't mean we don't have to do them anyway. Probably, the first thing to do is decide if the activity is really necessary in the student's day. (For example: If a student really dislikes putting on earphones, is it necessary that he listen to earphones during a certain time slot, or can that be replaced with another activity?) Of course, there are many activities of daily life which can not or should not be eliminated. In those instances, try letting the student know what is going to happen and also what will happen after. Getting him to focus on the desirable second activity can often get him to participate and endure what he doesn't like. Keep a visual symbol of that desirable activity close so you can refer to it regularly during the disliked activity. Have the student look at it, hold it, point to it, carry it, or whatever will help him look ahead to what he really wants to do. This diversionary tactic has helped work through lots of difficult times.

Let's see how this transition stuff all works.

SAMPLES & EXAMPLES

PROBLEM: Donald loved to go to gym. When he would leave the classroom he assumed he was going to gym. If the teacher decided to take Donald to accompany her to the office, there was always a problem. They walked down the hallway to a point where there is a fork. To go right is the gym. The office is left. Donald would start to go right and if the teacher would try to steer him to the left, a "lay down on the floor" temper tantrum would ensue.

SOLUTION: It was obvious that Donald needed more information when leaving the classroom. The teacher posted several pictures by the classroom door. They were pictures of locations in the school building: gym, office, bathroom, lunch room, storage closet, etc. When they were leaving the classroom, Donald was given a picture that represented their destination. He carried the picture throughout his trip and the teacher repeatedly reinforced the connection between the picture and the location. Donald's traveling behavior improved when he better understood his destinations.

A simple help for these circumstances is to have a collection of pictures of places to go. Use a visual tool to give information about your destination when leaving the classroom, the school building, or when leaving home in the car.

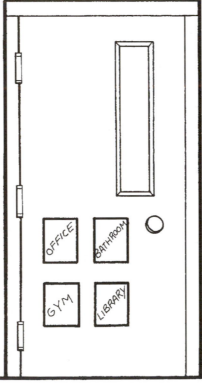

For some students, this might make the difference between a successful or unsuccessful trip to a less familiar environment (i.e., dentist). Other students handle transitions most of the time, but on a bad day it is a disaster. Another group of students are affected by transitions regardless of the time or destination. One approach to help the students understand this procedure is to introduce visual tools for both those regular, familiar situations and the variations. That way, the routine can be established for getting information from the visual tools. When the potentially difficult circumstance arises, the routine will be familiar.

PROBLEM: Kyle's mother attempts to take him with her when she does her Saturday morning shopping. She does not follow a set routine, but shops at different stores, depending on her needs. When they drive past certain stores Kyle becomes upset if she doesn't stop.

SOLUTION: Creating a little book of pictures of the typical places they stop (grocery store, dry cleaners, hardware store, etc.) helped Kyle's mother give him more information during their travels. She opened the book to show Kyle the picture of where they were going next. Seeing where they were going helped Kyle understand better than if she just told him. Mom also put pictures of Kyle's favorite fast food restaurant and a couple of treats in the book. If the plan was to make two stops and then stop for lunch, Mom could rearrange the pictures to show Kyle the sequence of events for that excursion, creating a mini-schedule.

hamburger

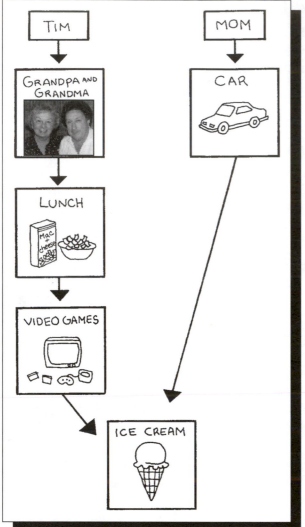

Tim is going to Grandma and Grandpa's house. Tim will eat lunch. Tim will play video games. Mom will go shopping in the car. When Mom comes back Tim and Mom will go for ice cream.

PROBLEM: Tim's family goes to visit Grandma and Grandpa regularly. Sometimes Mom leaves Tim there for Grandma to baby-sit. Tim doesn't like to be left at Grandma's. If Tim senses or figures out that they are going to Grandma's, he displays a large protest because he associates going to Grandma's with being left there. Mom doesn't want to tell him ahead of time where they are going because she fears his negative behavior.

SOLUTION: Tell him. In a visual way, let him know that they are going to Grandma's but Mom is not going to leave him there. On the days that Grandma will baby-sit, tell him that, too. If Tim knows what is going to happen, that should begin to eliminate problems. On the days that Mom will stay with Tim, he will understand he is not being left and should go more willingly. Then on the days that Mom will leave him, try some supportive strategies. Tell Tim when Mom will return, or tell him what will happen when she returns, or give him a schedule of events while he is at Grandma's, or reward his good behavior with a desirable choice. It might be necessary to try some techniques to figure out what has meaning for Tim. The biggest challenge is identifying *why* Tim doesn't like to be left at Grandma's. Then use that understanding to develop ways to give him information.

REMEMBER: Transition and travel times have a high potential for being problem times. There can be a variety of reasons for the problems to occur. Understanding *why* the student reactions are occurring is the beginning. Giving information in a visual form won't solve all the problems, however, many potentially difficult situations can be avoided or modified by employing this technique.

THE POINT IS: Using visual strategies to support transitions and travel between environments:

- clarifies what is ending and what is beginning
- gives students specific information about what to expect
- provides a concrete reference that the student can keep returning to as many times as necessary
- can help eliminate many behavior problems that erupt during transitions

Chapter 3

Aids To Give Effective Directions

A major challenge when working with students is giving instructions and directions in ways that facilitate a smooth flow of activity through the day. In addition, those in charge must divide their time to support the multiple student needs that develop. The average classroom will have at least a few students who require more teacher time and attention than the others, regardless of what student abilities are present. Those with more severe learning needs earn reputations of needing "one-on-one-individual attention," a commodity that is frequently more easily stated than provided.

Some days it feels as if I have a whole class of students who need "one-on-one" attention. I am exhausted!

One educational goal for all students should be to give them the structure and skills necessary to function as independently as possible. Teaching students to be dependent on constant adult intervention or supervision is not desirable.

Reducing verbal output to match the student's comprehension level is critical for effective communication. Measure his comprehension level by the consistency of his performance. If he responds consistently when he hears sentences, then use them. If he needs one word directions to respond appropriately, then that is the level of language that should be used. One of the most common reasons for student lack of performance is because the language environment is too advanced for the student.

In the typical classroom, the majority of directions are given verbally. It is not unusual for teachers to need to repeat them many times and to redirect students repeatedly. Visual supports help teachers accomplish their goal with much less effort.

I would love for them to be more independent, but they're not. How do I do this?

Develop a classroom style of using visual aids to support teacher directions and instruction.

The visual supports will help the *students* to:

- establish and maintain attention
- stay focused to get complete instructions
- clarify instructions
- perform to completion

The visual supports will help the *teachers*:

- by using less time for repetition of directions and instructions
- by reducing the intensity of support needed for many students
- be consistent with training procedures
- be consistent with the language used for verbal requests and directions
- plan ahead for more specific and organized presentations to the students

The use of visual supports can dramatically affect overall classroom management. Once you make a decision that visual strategies have value for your classroom, you will see endless ways to incorporate that visual element into the ongoing program.

CLASSROOM MANAGEMENT TOOLS

CLASSROOM MANAGEMENT TOOLS are specifically designed for the teacher to communicate more effectively *to* the students. They support both routine and unique communications that the teacher uses during daily activities. The focus of classroom management tools is to support those communications that the teacher uses to direct student movement and basic instruction. These are the *teacher's* communication tools; used to support the things the teacher tells the students. There are many benefits derived from the use of these visual supports.

Gain and maintain student attention

It is often easier for students to establish visual attention, especially in classrooms or environments where there is a lot of noisy activity. For those who are easily distracted, losing and then reestablishing attention can result in missing a large portion of the message being communicated. If a familiar visual support is a part of the communication interaction, the student can more quickly reestablish attention and comprehend what is being said.

Create support for students to stay on task, using less teacher intervention

When students are off task, not paying attention, not following through a sequence of actions, or not doing what they are supposed to be doing, the natural response is for the teacher to increase verbal correction and redirection. The more the student is not doing what he should be doing, the more the teacher talks. Student attention and comprehension can be supported without bombarding with more verbal input, by employing nonverbal visual strategies, including:

- gestures
- facial expressions
- physical prompting
- pointing to things in the environment
- showing visual tools
- other nonverbal visual prompts

Students can actually come to rely on excessive verbal prompting to accomplish their goals. It is a form of *learned dependence*. They learn to wait for more verbal direction, as if engaged in a turn taking interaction. The student waits for the teacher to take a turn by giving a direction. Then the student's turn is to perform an action. Then the student waits for the teacher to take a turn, and the turn taking continues. Besides being less distracting, nonverbal cues are easier to fade than verbal cues as students gradually develop more independence.

Make directions very clear and concise

Significant numbers of students who experience communication handicaps require less, not more, teacher verbalization. Although some language development theories encourage the use of expanding the verbalization used to instruct students, that technique does not prove effective with our targeted students. Reducing the language-uncomplicating the auditory environment-produces positive results for many. Write on the aid exactly what you say when you are using it. That will help you use more succinct language. Classroom management aids encourage all those interacting with the students to reduce their language to similar, simple phrases.

> *There is a training strategy that suggests "building up" the language you use with students so they will increase their language understanding and use. It is important, however, to begin at the student's real comprehension level and build up one step at a time. Too often, people start higher than the student is capable of handling or build up too fast. Because students learn to follow familiar routines, they can give the appearance of understanding more than they really do.*

"Sit down in the red chair" becomes *"sit"*

"Come over to the circle and sit on the floor" becomes *"come"* or *"sit in the circle"*

"Go out to your locker and get your lunch" becomes *"get your lunch"*

"It's not nice to hit. You had better keep your hands to yourself" becomes *"quiet hands"*

The process of creating classroom management tools helps teachers weed out wordiness and focus on those communications most essential for effective classroom management. Putting the communications in a visual form encourages continuity among the variety of people directing those students.

Encourage simple, routine communications

It is not uncommon to say the same things in many different ways. Communication consistency, however, benefits many students. This does not mean everyone in the child's life needs to speak from an exact script, but attaching consistent verbal routines to the performance routines that students are learning will enhance the overall process.

Help students remember what needs to be remembered

Students *do* need reminding and redirection and prompting of various sorts. When using the visual tools, students learn to attend to and access them to manage themselves more independently. When classroom structures are set up to encourage students to do what they need to do with as little adult intervention as possible, the result will be an overall atmosphere that is more flowing, organized and congenial.

I like the idea of using visual tools to help me give students directions, but how could I possibly do it? I talk all day. It would be impossible to put all of that in visual form!

At first, the thought of visually representing everything a teacher says during the course of a day can appear to be an overwhelming task. The average teacher says a lot! Luckily, the task becomes simpler once you begin to organize your needs. The development of classroom management tools should evolve around specific needs or activities that are identified.

It would not be easy to log everything that is communicated in a classroom in a day. On the other hand, it is a fairly simple task for most teachers to list some of those things that they have to repeat many, many times during the course of a day. That is the place to begin looking for visual possibilities.

Keep some paper close so you can write down ideas as they occur throughout the day. There could be one list for overall classroom commands and another list that contains what is necessary to manage specific students. Then, think of how you handle special activities or subjects. There will be some natural overlap between the teacher's classroom management language and the classroom rules or the visual tools developed for other purposes. The overlap is not a problem. What we call these tools is not as important as the fact that they are being established to assist in supporting communication. Classroom management tools belong to the teacher to support talking to the students. With that mind set, the possibilities become more clear.

> *Establishing a core set of directions to guide a targeted student is an effective strategy, particularly when he is in an environment where a variety of people are in charge. A classroom where there are teachers aides and ancillary staff; home with parents, siblings, baby sitters; a group home or living situation where there are rotating staff to supervise students are all situations where coordination will result in improvement.*

potato masher

CaKe Mix VANILLA

milk

Frosting CHOCOLATE

eggs

bowl

pan

spatula

SAMPLES & EXAMPLES

PROBLEM: The class was involved in a cooking activity. The teacher asked Joe to bring the milk from the refrigerator. Joe got up from his chair, walked to the fan to watch it spin and paid attention to several other distractions on his way to the refrigerator. When he opened the refrigerator door, he reached in, with eyes on the ceiling, and happened to grab the butter which he brought back to the work table. During this episode, much teacher language was used to redirect Joe to the task at hand. It didn't help.

SOLUTION: The teacher developed a set of object cards that represent items needed in the cooking routine. When she asked Joe to get an item, she handed him a card with that item on it. Joe looked at the card while he walked across the room. When he reached the refrigerator he looked at the card again to remember what he was supposed to retrieve. He selected the correct item and brought it back. Joe completed the task independently so the teacher could attend to other group needs.

PROBLEM: Classroom transition times are difficult. The teacher experiences difficulty trying to get everybody to do what they are supposed to do. They all seem to need attention at the same time. Everyone forgets what they were told or what they are supposed to do. If the teacher gives individual directions to students, they are unable to differentiate which ones are for them and which for their classmates. One particularly difficult time is when the students are moving from a group activity to snack time.

SOLUTION: Develop a set of cards that assign the different tasks to be accomplished during the transition. Give each student a card that specifically directs what he should do during that time. The students will be more focused as the transition time becomes more organized. It is easier to monitor and remember what everyone is supposed to be doing if directions are supported visually.

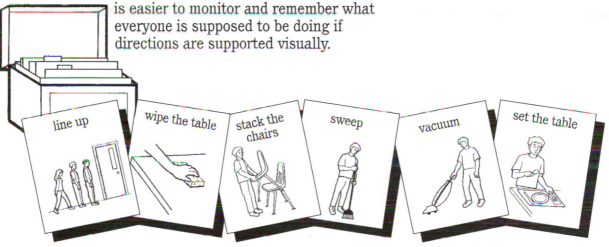

When selecting visuals, choose what the students will recognize quickly and easily.

DEVELOPING CLASSROOM MANAGEMENT TOOLS

What should these tools look like? What format do you recommend?

Since these tools are used in a way that requires rapid recognition, a combination of pictures and words generally is most effective. The type of pictures selected should be recognized by the students as quickly and easily as possible. Size and mobility of these tools are significant factors to consider when developing them since it is essential that they be convenient to use for the functioning style of the classroom.

Some pictures are commercially available in 2" sizes or smaller. Even though they are published in those smaller sizes, that may not be the best size for your student's efficient comprehension. Using pictures that are the wrong size for a student can cause a system to fail.

Big pictures: Younger students, those who have more difficulty establishing attention, or those who are just learning to recognize pictures frequently respond to bigger formats. Some students don't appear very interested in smaller pictures (i.e., 2x2 or 3 1/2 x 5), but will respond more consistently to larger sizes (i.e., 5x7, 8x10 or larger). Big pictures work better if students need to see them from far away or if several students need to see them at once. Experiment with size to see what works best for your students.

Little pictures: Many teacher tools serve their function conveniently if they are small or portable, and easy to manipulate. Smaller formats are easier to carry and don't take up so much room if you set them on a desk or table for a student.

It sounds like my organizational skills will be challenged. Where do I need to start?

Consider these options:

Teacher mini-book: Using a small book like a pocket size photo album, put each communication picture on a separate page to be opened and shown when needed. If the book fits into the teacher's pocket it can be retrieved easily when needed. A teacher book may contain some generic items used across the day; student rules and directions for class movement. A separate book may be developed to assist with needs for a targeted activity or location. You may find that your communication is very activity specific. For example: Separate communication needs are identified for 1)the lunchroom, 2)gym, 3)going shopping and 4)riding the bus. Try creating a separate mini-book for each activity.

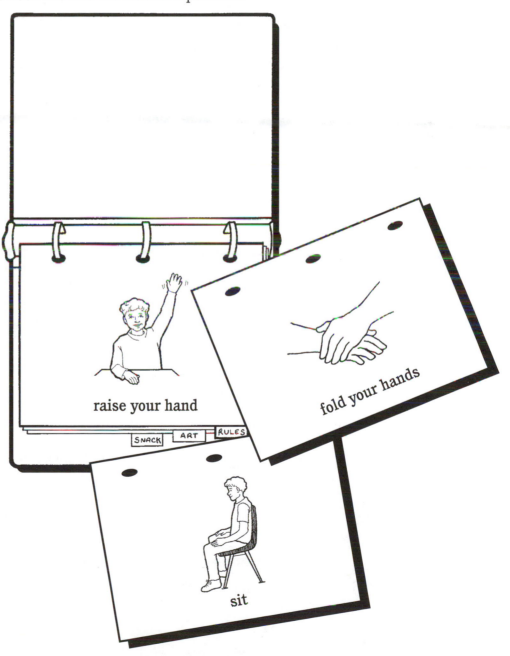

		O.T.
Brushing	Swings	Balance Beam
Spinner	Ball	Exercise
Platform Swing	Stairs	Scooter Board

Teacher notebook: To avoid several smaller items, another option is to use a 3-ring binder. The larger page format can contain pages that are each developed for a specific activity or special time. Although some find the larger format cumbersome, others find the big book harder to lose. The large book can be opened and laid on a table or work area to be used with individuals or small groups of students. The larger visuals are great for showing a group of students.

Picture card files: A collection of pictures of objects needed and steps or directions given during specific training activities will assist, particularly with activities where the teacher may give different directions to each student or when the directions vary from session to session. This collection can have cards to support very specific routines that have been established.

		ART
crayons	markers	paper
paint	paint brush	pencil
water	sponge	scissors

THE POINT IS: Using visual tools to manage classroom communication:

- increases the effectiveness of teacher communication

- helps students perform more consistently

- makes the communication process more efficient for everyone involved

TASK ORGANIZERS AND COOKBOOKS

There are many students who have learned how to perform parts of a job or activity, yet lack the ability to complete the whole task or sequence of steps independently. Perhaps they forget in which order the steps occur, they get distracted and eliminate steps, or they get confused or just can't remember what to do next. For others, their lack of independence is the result of a learned dependency; the byproduct of teaching procedures that inadvertently encouraged it.

TASK ORGANIZERS and **COOKBOOKS** are step by step prompts to help a student complete a task more independently. Just as the chef needs to go to the cookbook to find and follow a recipe, many students need a similar set of cues to assist them in successfully accomplishing a task.

I understand. This technique is for cooking class. We can use it when we cook every Friday.

Don't limit yourself. This concept works for accomplishing many types of tasks, not just cooking. The performance of any job that requires several steps to complete can be enhanced for those students who need that extra assistance.

> *Task organizers and cookbooks are not just for cooking activities. They work for any activity that requires several steps to complete a task.*

Sometimes I think the teaching staff are the ones who have the problems. My aide and I found out that we were teaching some skills very differently. No wonder the students were confused!

That is a frequent problem. It is not uncommon to find that each teacher or caregiver will use different methods or sequences to accomplish the same task. Even when specific procedures are agreed upon, there can be a tendency to personalize them. Some trainers will continually vary the methods or task sequence for teaching skills without evaluating the consequences of the changes or sharing those changes with others who are teaching those skills. Variations in the training procedures can inadvertently lengthen the time necessary for students to learn skills, particularly when training students who learn more slowly. These task organizers and cookbooks help provide a systematic, organized and consistent way of teaching the steps to complete tasks. They provide the opportunity for "error free" learning.

What do you mean by "error free" learning?

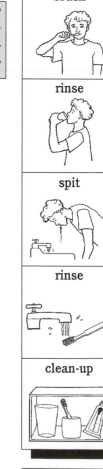

Which goal is preferable?
Performing a few tasks without
supports or performing a larger
number of tasks with supports?

That means providing such a highly structured learning experience, that the students literally do not have the opportunity to make mistakes. Using the visual tools, you show them what the next step is and you prompt them, if necessary, to follow that step. Then you show them the next step and prompt as necessary. By using this procedure, the students have the opportunity to perform all the steps of a task without "guessing" what is supposed to come next and without making mistakes. As the student practices the task repeatedly, any prompting can gradually be reduced, leaving the visual tool to guide the student through the steps. The student learns to refer to the visual tool as a part of the routine, so he actually prompts himself through the task. Performing the routine the same way consistently results in more rapid learning.

But what if the students learn to depend on the visual tools? Will they always need to use these cookbooks and task organizers to accomplish the tasks? That wouldn't be good, would it?

Some students will use the tools until they have memorized the procedures. Then they will not need to use the tools any more. Others will continue to use the tools forever, for the structure and organization, to successfully stay on task to complete their goals. It is just like the cook who has some recipes memorized and needs the cookbook for others. Either way works. What is important is the end result.

SAMPLES & EXAMPLES

PROBLEM: Jack can perform pieces of his daily personal grooming activities. He knows how to brush his teeth. When he is sent to brush, he invariably forgets to do at least one of the necessaries. It is typical for him to get stuck at one of the steps and just kind of stay there until someone comes to prompt him to complete the task.

SOLUTION: Create a chart that lists all the steps to be done. Teach Jack to follow the sequence of activities on the chart so he can complete the whole task.

Task Organizers and Cookbooks

PROBLEM: Stu loves to work in the kitchen. He is developing considerable skill in helping prepare several of his favorite snack foods. His teachers feel he could learn to prepare the snacks independently if he could remember what to do and when to do it. With some structure, he could be successful.

SOLUTION: Prepare task organizers or cookbooks that contain the steps necessary for Jack and Stu to accomplish their goals. Teach them to follow the steps.

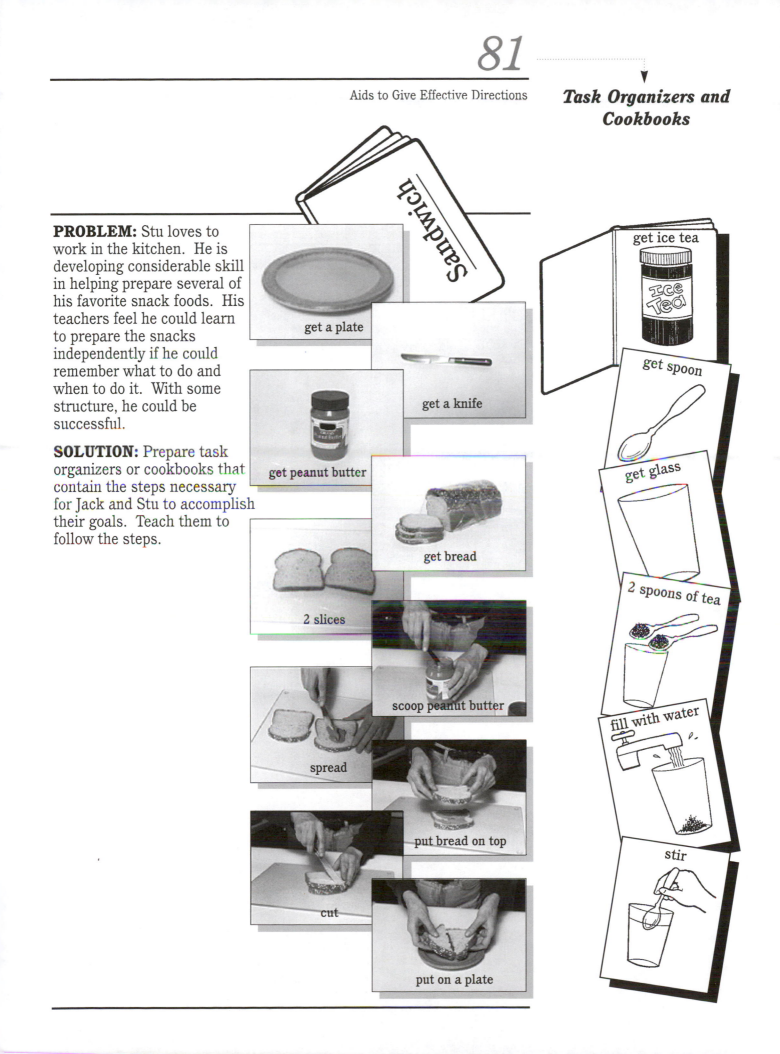

Sandwich

get a plate

get a knife

get peanut butter

get bread

2 slices

scoop peanut butter

spread

put bread on top

cut

put on a plate

get ice tea

get spoon

get glass

2 spoons of tea

fill with water

stir

Task Organizers and Cookbooks

PROBLEM: When the students begin doing independent work in the classroom, there is a considerable amount of confusion. All the students seem to need individual attention to help them get their materials to begin working. The teacher has difficulty giving the students the individual attention they appear to need all at the same time.

SOLUTION: Develop task organizers that direct students to assemble their own materials to perform their individual jobs.

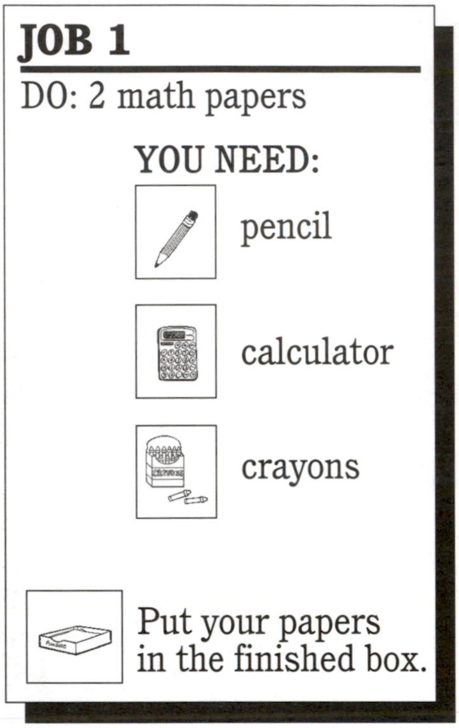

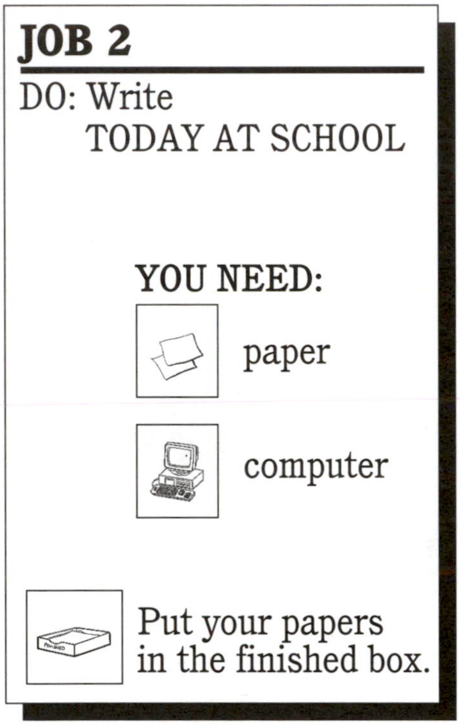

JOB 1
DO: 2 math papers
YOU NEED:
pencil
calculator
crayons
Put your papers in the finished box.

JOB 2
DO: Write
TODAY AT SCHOOL
YOU NEED:
paper
computer
Put your papers in the finished box.

PROBLEM: The teacher gives the students an art task or some other activity that involves several steps. Invariably several students forget which step to do in which order. They glue before they cut or some other mix-up. The result is a sticky heap that doesn't resemble the original goal.

SOLUTION: Create a prompt card where students can refer to help guide themselves through the steps. Refer students to the prompt card to discover what to do next.

1. color

2. cut

3. glue

DON'T FORGET!

back pack

jacket

lunch box

hat

note book

mittens

money

PROBLEM: Jerry rushes through transition times without remembering what his responsibilities are during that transition. When arriving at school he heads straight for his favorite game, forgetting that he has to hang up his coat, give notes to the teacher, and several other steps that are part of the arrival routine. When it is time to go home he attempts to head out the door before collecting his belongings and following the departure routines. Getting ready to leave home for school in the morning is a chaotic interlude with Jerry running back and forth to remember things...or rather Jerry's mom running back and forth to try to get him to remember things.

PROBLEM: Phil also demonstrates difficulty during the transition times. He is apt to stand there..forever..not remembering what to do next. Then he will stare at the ceiling, or get distracted by some oddity, such as a fan or knob. Phil will need to be redirected many times to follow the routine.

SOLUTION: Create some mini task organizers to assist Jerry and Phil through the difficult transition times in the day. Teach them to look at the "check list" of tasks to remember what to do. Hang that check list in a location where it will catch their attention and be a convenient reference.

CREATING TASK ORGANIZERS AND COOKBOOKS

1. LIST ALL THE MATERIALS NECESSARY

For a cooking task, think of all the ingredients and utensils necessary. For non-cooking tasks, include materials students would have to retrieve to complete the job.

2. LIST, IN ORDER, THE STEPS NECESSARY TO ACCOMPLISH THE TASK

Think carefully about what order the steps should occur to make the task most simple or efficient for the students. For example: If making a grilled cheese sandwich, do you put the cheese in the bread first and then butter the bread, or do you butter the bread and then put the cheese in between. Do you butter both sides of the bread before putting the sandwich in the frying pan, or do you put the sandwich into the pan before buttering the second piece of bread?

Will it help the student if he accomplishes one step before another? Should he put on his coat first or get his school bag first? Brush his teeth first or wash his face first? Does he need to cut or color or paste first?

3. SELECT THE ESSENTIAL STEPS

Different levels of detail may be needed for different students. For some students, just a few key steps are necessary; the other steps are assumed. That means the student will automatically do them. For example, when making cookies from a box mix, if the direction says "pour the cookie mix in the bowl," most students will assume the step of opening the box to dump the mix in the bowl. There are other students who may need more of those assumed steps to be added to a sequence.

4. DECIDE WHERE IN THE SEQUENCE IT WOULD BE MOST EFFICIENT FOR THE STUDENT TO ASSEMBLE NEEDED MATERIALS

For some students it is better to assemble all materials or ingredients before beginning the task. For other students it may be more natural to get the utensils or supplies at the point in the task when they are needed. If a student is working on a task where he will need scissors in the middle, should he get them at the beginning of his work and leave them on the table until he is ready for them, or is he better able to focus on his task with the scissors in another location until he is ready for them?

5. SELECT A REPRESENTATION SYSTEM

Written words, labeled pictures, photographs, or a combination of these can be successful. When using picture and photo systems, write on them exactly what you call the items or what you say for the student to complete the step.

6. SELECT A FORMAT and LOCATION

The natural inclination of classroom teachers is to make charts to hang on walls. That may not be the most effective form. Smaller formats that are mobile and can be used on a table or desk are more convenient in many settings. Some students benefit from carrying an organizer in the pocket to be pulled out at the appropriate time. Other reminders should be stored in the specific location where they will be used.

TRAINING TO USE TASK ORGANIZERS AND COOKBOOKS

When I decide to use these visual tools, do I just give them to the student? Do you have any recommendations for how to teach a student to use them?

Just giving one of these tools to the student is not enough. It is essential to teach him how to use it efficiently. Once he learns what to do, your teaching job is much easier.

It is important to be aware of how you direct or prompt students through the process. Here are some suggestions that will enable teachers to train students for independence.

1. Direct student's attention to the visual aid.

2. Limit verbal prompting. State the verbal script for each step. If the student needs more assistance, repeat the verbal script.

3. Further prompting, if necessary, should involve gestures (pointing to visual aid or guiding and pointing to materials), modeling (demonstrating the step), or physical guidance (place trainer's hand over student's hand while assisting completion of the step).

4. If the student is verbal, encourage him to verbalize each step in the process. Repeating the verbal script is a helpful part of the routine. When students learn to say or think the verbal script that guides the routine, it becomes a self-talk or self-prompt to direct their own behavior.

5. Guide the student's attention back to the visual aid after each step is accomplished. Show him how to move to the next step by turning a page or pointing to the next item in the list of steps.

6. As the student becomes more familiar with the task, both verbal prompting and nonverbal prompts should gradually be reduced. If the student gets off task or appears to need direction, guide his attention back to the visual aid for his prompt.

7. As the student learns to perform the task more independently, some of the training steps that were originally identified may become assumed steps. At that point it is appropriate to eliminate those cues from the visual sequence. It may be appropriate to change the number of steps in the visual sequence as the student learns the task.

If we are aiming toward independence, doesn't that mean we should work toward eliminating the visual tools?

When students begin to acquire more skill, some teachers are very eager to remove the visual tools completely....assuming that students are functioning on a higher level when not using it. As a result, removal of the visual tools becomes a goal. *CAUTION* is advised here. Some students will eventually be able to accomplish their routines without support. Others continue to have long term needs for the visual supports. Consider these groups of students:

> **Group 1:** Students who use the tools while they are learning the steps of a routine. Once the routine is mastered, they really don't require the support any more.

> **Group 2:** Students who benefit from the tools to help them focus their attention on the task at hand, organize their behavior, and remember what to do. These students may always benefit from the support.

> **Group 3:** Students who display inconsistent behavior or have ups and downs (don't we all?). They will not appear to need to use the tools in the "up" times. Continuing to use the tools, however, provides a consistent routine so when these students experience difficult days, the familiar visual tools help support them through their routines.

Frequently, the presence of the visual aids is a long term strategy to help students accomplish what they are supposed to do. After tasks are practiced and learned, the tools may not be used in the same manner as when they were first introduced, but *they have not lost their usefulness.* They still have meaning to the student.

What does not seem to work is to put the visual tools away in a drawer somewhere, pulled out only when a student is having a bad day. They need to be out and available and integrated as a regular part of the student's educational environment. Observation of the student's performance will guide the decisions.

REMEMBER: The key goal is to train the student to use the cookbook or task organizer to get his information and prompting rather than encouraging reliance on the teacher.

Visual aids can be implemented as short term helps toward accomplishing a goal. They can be developed as long term supporting strategies for a specific environment or for performance of a targeted routine.

As a student becomes familiar with an organizational system he may change the way he responds to it. Just because he doesn't use visual supports in the same way he did when they were introduced, that is not a signal to eliminate them. Think of it this way: what would happen if the traffic signs were eliminated from your neighborhood? Do you think drivers would change how they drive?

Food for Thought: If a task is too complicated to put in a visual form, does that mean it is too complicated to teach?

Why do you suggest limiting verbal prompting?

If the trainer uses a lot of verbal prompting it will be difficult to reduce his or her presence. Many students develop a dependency on turn taking with trainers. This is how they perceive the process: the trainer takes a turn telling me what to do, I take a turn doing something, the trainer take a turn telling me what to do and then I take a turn doing something, and on and on.

Other students haven't learned how to really think about what they are doing. They are so dependent on the verbal cues to tell them what to do that they don't think through the steps to figure out "where am I in this sequence?" Their actions are impulsive rather than thoughtful or logical. Visual cues can work better than verbal prompting to guide them through the thinking process.

Some of the things I have my students do would be too hard to represent visually. The tasks are too complicated to put in visual form.

Good point! When teachers begin to analyze how many steps are involved in some of the sequences they are teaching, they become more aware of the complexity of their requirements for their students. Without even realizing it, we can become frustrated with students who don't master ten step sequences, when in reality those students may even have difficulty staying on task for two. Problems occur, in part, because we aren't even aware that the tasks we are attempting are as complicated as they actually are. For example, when selecting menu items for students to cook, grilled cheese may come to mind because it is "kid's food." Think about how many more steps are involved in making a grilled cheese sandwich than in making a bologna sandwich. A transition time like getting ready to go home may easily contain ten or more steps. No wonder some students get lost along the way. Careful observation will give you information to guide your planning. Just remember, start simple. It will result in faster learning and a sense of accomplishment for all involved.

INSTRUCTION OF NEW MATERIAL

Preparing ahead for teaching a new task with visual supports will be well worth the time. Depending on the task, a teacher tool, a task organizer or cookbook might be the choice.

That means I need to prepare the tool before I begin to teach the activity. How will I know what to put in it if I haven't seen the student do the task?

When to prepare the visuals is a question that is not answered simply. Really organized people would advocate for putting the tool together before presenting the task to the student. Preparing ahead of time will produce a less confusing introduction to the new task. The shortcoming to this procedure is discovering you have taken a lot of time to prepare gorgeous visuals for a new task and then realizing it doesn't meet the student's need adequately.

The way you approach this dilemma will depend on how well you know the student. Consider these options:

- Do a "run through" of the task with the student to observe what parts he is able to do.

- Partially prepare your visual tools ahead; create a rough draft. Then, run through the procedures to see if you have targeted the points you need to represent visually. Make these tools in formats that can be changed easily so you can make modifications as needed.

- Prepare the visuals while the teaching is going on. Keeping a camera, pencil and paper, or chalk for the chalkboard handy, make a visual prompt when the need arises while the student is watching. This often generates much attention from the students and creates a meaningful association for them.

Whichever way you begin, just remember, teaching new skills becomes easier when visual tools are employed to help the process.

> CONSIDER THIS: *The process of putting a task in visual form will simplify your teaching procedures.*

SUGGESTIONS FOR GIVING DIRECTIONS EFFECTIVELY

Encourage everyone to use the visual aids, not just teacher.
Students will generally respond best to the people they are most familiar with. Their performance may change for teacher's aides, baby sitters, bus drivers, lunch ladies, ancillary staff, substitute teachers or anyone else who is in the position to interact with them. Consider how to expand the use of visual aids to others in the student's environment.

Write on the aid exactly what you say.
This will encourage simple, concrete language. In addition, it will encourage continuity among people. Using consistent language is helpful to students.

Don't use "pidgin" English. Use simple language, but use phrases that sound grammatically and prosodically normal.
Comprehension of language is enhanced by the prosodic elements (the flow of the speech). Making language sound abnormal will not improve the student's comprehension.

Choose flexible formats.
Classroom aids are likely to require changing from time to time to meet the changing student needs. Aids that are changed to meet those new student requirements will be the most effective. A tool in a "rough draft" form, that can be changed easily, might work better than the one that is perfectly laminated and can't be modified.

Make sure the aids are conveniently available.
If you have to look for them or they are in another room or they are under a pile of "stuff" they won't be useful. Teachers who identify specific "homes" for the various tools are not frequently frustrated from losing them.

Once you develop the use of visual systems, be careful about eliminating the aids from your program.
Teachers who have reported experiencing great success from using the aids have sometimes gradually or arbitrarily eliminated using the aids as students progressed. Some of these teachers have later reported that targeted students have "regressed" or reverted to old behavior and performance patterns. Analysis of the situations has revealed that as the students learned the skills more independently, the teacher gradually got out of the pattern of using the tools. Even though the students didn't seem to need the visual aids in the same way they did when they first began to use them, when the aids were totally eliminated from the program, the student's improved performance was not maintained. Either old behavior resurfaced or teachers gradually began verbally prompting more and more.

THE POINT IS: Using visual tools to help give directions:

- helps gain and maintain student attention

- makes the teaching of a task more routine or consistent

- standardizes directions and procedures among various teachers and caregivers

- helps students learn to perform sequences faster

- increases student reliability and consistency

- gives students a greater sense of independence

- helps students stay on task

- helps students work through behavior problems

- enables students to perform more complicated or lengthy tasks with less supervision

REMEMBER: Most teachers find that the visual tools they employ to manage classroom activities will change as the year goes on. Creating these in formats that are easily changeable proves to be most effective.

Chapter 4

Visual Strategies To Organize The Environment

Organization style is a highly personal trait. People range from the rigid to the chaotic on this one. If each person observes his own life, he can probably identify a wide range of techniques that give his life a sense of order and some areas of tolerance that allow disorder. Think about your own functioning style. Do you have a pile of important "stuff" sitting on your kitchen counter or your desk? Can you easily find your cookware or tools when needed? Would you be able to retrieve a piece of mail you received a couple of months ago? What about your car keys? Do you always know where they are? What kind of rituals and rules have you built into your own living and working environment to help you function more efficiently?

Have you been watching me? I do have a unique style of piling and losing things! But I always know where my car keys are. What does this have to do with teaching my students?

Part of the educational process is to teach, or allow students to discover, systems and tools that will be a helpful part of their own personal management style. Many students with autism or other learning problems have a built in rigidity that dictates a non-flexible way of coping with their environments. Comprehending their need for predictability makes the rigidity more understandable. Working *with* that need for organization can produce some environmental adaptations that will result in less rigidity but more comfortable comprehension and relaxed functioning. As they learn to make use of the organizational possibilities around them, students become more efficient. They *like* the structure and organization.

I want to give them that structure, but it is hard because I am not like that. I am more spontaneous and disorganized. Is there hope for me?

A classroom or living environment can be set up to provide lots of built-in structure. Working toward that goal will probably benefit both you and the students as you coexist. Finished papers go in this box. That toy goes on the shelf in this exact spot. The cups go on the first shelf and the plates go on the second shelf. Using visual cues to help organize the environment will make that organizational system more clear to everyone using it. In addition, the visual tools assist with teaching changes that will inevitably occur.

Students who experience learning difficulties usually demonstrate a need for structure and for learning organizational strategies. Supporting them is this area results in major improvements in their overall performance.

STRUCTURING THE ENVIRONMENT WITH LABELING

Our world is full of visual elements to give people cues to function efficiently. Bathrooms are labeled. So are exits. Rooms and school busses are given numbers. Students benefit from being taught to identify already existing environmental cues. In addition, home and school environments can be visually enhanced to give students more information. Adding labels and markers provides an opportunity for more independence than a student might otherwise be able to accomplish. Try these techniques.

Teach students to recognize the labels and information that already occur naturally in the environment

Many labels are already there. That does not mean students recognize them or know what they mean. It does not mean students will know how to act upon the information. Many students need to be specifically taught how to make use of environmental supports.

Label the student's personal spaces and personal belongings

The most common forms of labeling are putting student's names on coat racks, desks, chairs, mail box, lockers, and lunch box locations. Students are helped when labels identify their lunch boxes, coats, gym clothes, and all those personal possessions.

> Remember to teach students to get information from the visual cues that already occur in the environment.

> Teaching students to identify and effectively use the visual cues in their environments is an important part of communication training. Recognizing or reading these cues does not insure the ability to act appropriately upon the messages conveyed. That is the communication part. Reading these cues out of context is an insignificant skill. Recognizing them and then demonstrating an understanding of what they mean by acting on the information correctly is what is critical.

Label where things belong

Labeling can show where items belong on a shelf, what is in drawers, or cabinets, and where finished work should be put. The finished work goes in a specific box, the art supplies belong in identified containers, and the toys go in designated places on the shelves.

Label the environment

Use labeling to help articulate the organization of the child's whole program. Give a name to all activities and label the various activity areas in and out of the classroom. For example, give specific names to tables or areas of a classroom where specific activities take place:

- the art table
- the round table
- the work table
- the good morning circle
- the book corner

- the play rug
- the leisure area
- the break area

> *Many developmental curriculums list matching as an important skill to learn. Replacing an object in a labeled drawer or putting a tool back on a labeled shelf is a functional performance of that skill. Using the labeling concept teaches the matching skill in a useful format, much more functional than matching lotto pictures.*

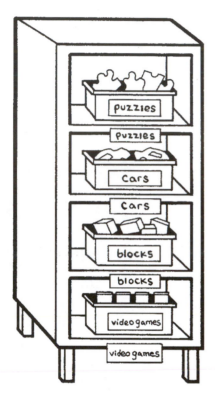

Coordinate those names and labels with the activity names used in the student's daily schedule. Students who experience difficulty with transitioning from one activity or location to the next are particularly assisted by this system. Here is how these organization strategies work.

SAMPLES & EXAMPLES

PROBLEM: Keeping the classroom organized is difficult. Students and staff all have different ideas about where things belong. The stapler is always missing and the students frequently lose their school supplies.

SOLUTION: Label everything. Identify locations for the stapler and other items. Label the locations and teach students to put items back in the labeled area. Teach the students to match the label with the item and show them how to put things away. When having the students retrieve items, show them how to attend to the label to access what they need.

Develop a holder, (i.e. a box with a lid) for each student to hold individual school supplies. Put a label on or in the lid of the box that identifies exactly what belongs in the box. The label on the lid can serve as:

- a prompt to help the student communicate about the supplies he has or needs

- a check list to inventory what is in the box

- a reminder about what is supposed to go in the box

PROBLEM: Jean has difficulty taking care of her belongings at home. Mom feels she could be more independent at managing her own things like cleaning her room and helping with laundry, but she needs a system.

SOLUTION: Label the locations of items that Jean needs to retrieve or put away. Label shelves for toys, drawers and closets for clothing. Find holders and containers such as boxes, dish pans, or laundry baskets for items. Label the containers so Jean will remember what goes into each one.

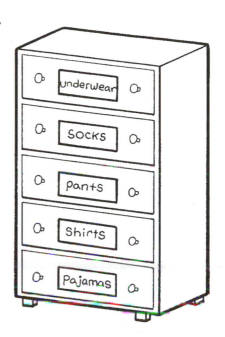

PROBLEM: Teddy requires much staff supervision while trying to accomplish a series of tasks. He seems to complete one task faster than his aide can get another one for him to do.

SOLUTION: Develop a system where Teddy can be more independent with the total routine by getting and putting away the materials he uses. Use a mini-schedule to list the activities or jobs Teddy will do. Place pictures or labels of the jobs in a holder. Put the activities into individual containers or baskets. Label the containers with the identical pictures. With a third set of pictures, label the shelves where the containers belong. Teach Teddy to look at his mini-schedule to identify what job he is supposed to take. When he completes his activity, he will be able to return his container to the proper place by looking for the identical label on the shelf and then move on to the next activity more independently.

REMEMBER: Just having the labels there is not enough. Most students will need to be taught how to use them. Teach them to find the cues, recognize them, and use the information from them.

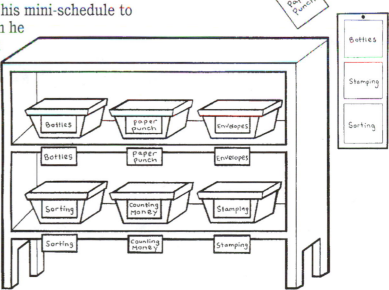

ORGANIZING LIFE IN GENERAL

There are lots more ways that life can be organized. Think about these opportunities.

SIGNS

Just as signs are used in the everyday world, highlighting procedures to function properly, they can be used in an educational environment to enhance a comfortable flow of life. Step one should be to teach students to attend to any already existing signs that would be meaningful to them. Step two is to add some signs to guide performance for specific locations or activities.

LISTS

Who has not created a shopping list or a list of "things to do" in our lives?

> *Students do not need to be able to write to make their own list. If they are not writers, try these:*
> - *dictate to someone*
> - *copy words on the computer*
> - *cut & paste pictures*
> - *circle items on a prepared sheet*

- Create a list for the student to use to help him accomplish a routine or activity.

- Guide the student through the procedure of creating his own list to accomplish a purpose. Teaching students to formulate their own version of a list can go a long way toward helping them to think through events in an organized fashion. It teaches them a strategy that is a life skill.

I like this idea. Besides shopping and things to do, what other kinds of lists do you recommend?

There are endless possibilities. Here are some suggestions:

things I must bring to school tomorrow: lunch money, a magazine

things I need to remember to take home today: note, homework, book, what I brought for show-&-tell

things to buy at the store: bread, peanut butter, paper towels

supplies to take to the laundromat: dirty clothes, laundry basket, soap, fabric softener, money

items to take to the swimming pool: bathing suit, towel, sandals, bathing cap, shampoo, recreation ID card

jobs to do to clean the bedroom: put shoes away, put toys on shelf, make bed, put clothes in hamper

tasks to do to prepare lunch: set table, make sandwiches, make beverage

things to do today: call for transportation, pay bills, go to the store

who to send cards to: birthday, Christmas, Valentine's

CHARTS

The classic "tooth brush chart" is not obsolete. Remembering anything on a daily or regular basis is much easier if there is a prompt to check or cross off. Remembering different activities on different days is enhanced even more by this procedure.

REMEMBERING AND GIVING MESSAGES

Writing something down or putting it in a visual form helps get a message delivered. How many phone messages have passed to oblivion because they didn't get recorded?

Think about how many opportunities a student has to transport a message between home and school or from one classroom to another. Teaching students to be responsible for delivering information is important. The *Today at School* concept is one form of this (see Mediating Communication Between Environments, Chapter 5). Students achieve more responsibility and independence when they learn to create and/or use visual prompts effectively to support them in the transfer of information from one person or environment to another.

MEMORY SUPPORTS

Did you ever help yourself remember to do something by putting a note on your bathroom mirror, in your pocket, by the handle of the door, or on the steering wheel of your car? Perhaps the classic is putting a note in your pocket. Students can benefit from those little reminders, too. Be creative!

REMEMBER: The key to teaching organizational strategies is to enable students to use these tools to develop a level of independence and consistent functioning. People might use a few of these strategies with students, however, there are probably many more opportunities in a student's life to develop tools to support organization. Frequently, organization systems are set up more for the adult in charge rather than considering them a strategic teaching tool for the students. It is less common to specifically teach the students to create their own organizational strategies. Teaching them how to create more structure for themselves can become a skill with lifetime value.

THE POINT IS: Organizing the environment with visual supports can:

- create an orderliness to the environment that gives students a sense of stability

- help students experience greater structure and predictability

- help students function more independently

- enable students to become more responsible for their own performance and belongings

- increase student reliability

- make it easier for everyone to find or remember what they need

Chapter 5

Mediating Communication Between Environments

One of the greatest desires of families, teachers, and friends of students who experience moderate to severe communication difficulties is to find out more about them and their life experiences. This information is what relationships are built upon.

When a student comes home from school to face a question like, "How was your day today?", lucky parents get a response that contains more than one word and gives them a bit of information about the time their child spent away from home. Most parents would desire more information than they get, however, those whose children experience communication handicaps have an even greater need. The more difficulty a student has in his ability to communicate, the greater the vacuum that exists about a large part of his life while he is away from home or away from school.

Teachers face the same dilemma. Great effort is often put into attempting to extract information from students about their experiences outside the classroom. Finding out what has happened in a student's life away from school is a necessary part of teaching meaningful communication. Any time these students cross over into other environments, the communication void can be wide.

What can I do? It takes a lot of time and effort to try to communicate with the families of my students. As hard as I try, I don't feel totally successful.

To fill the voids, teachers, parents, and other significant caretakers attempt to develop systems of exchanging information. These systems typically meet only part of the need. First, it can be time consuming and inconvenient to communicate by writing or telephoning with enough regularity to share all the details. Second, and most important, these systems generally do not include the student as a conduit of his own experience and information.

Do you have a better idea?

Teach students to communicate more information about themselves. **VISUAL BRIDGES** are designed to make that happen. Visual Bridges are communication tools that are developed from some combination of written words, pictures, objects or other visual cues. They are assembled to communicate information about the student's experience. They exist as a bridge to support the information exchange between two or more environments when the student is unable to handle the complete communication independently. They assist in stretching the student to a higher level of expression than he would be able to communicate without the support. Adaptable to any ability or age level, the system is ultimately a means of teaching students to communicate more information about themselves. Visual Bridges are different from other visual tools because they contain information that is immediate and activity specific. A new tool may be prepared on a daily basis to highlight today's most important information, or a tool can be created to share details about a specific event.

What do you try to accomplish by using Visual Bridges?

There are three major goals when implementing this system.

GOAL #1: mediate communication between home and school or other significant environments

The student is given the responsibility of sharing the information about himself. He learns more about sharing, telling, asking for information, and remembering things he needs to be responsible for. He learns to take more initiative for social interactions.

GOAL #2: stimulate and expand functional language, communication, reading & writing and academic development

The information is put in a visual form to help the transition from one environment to another. It is critical that the student participate as much as possible in the selection, creation, or production of the visual tools. His participation is part of the learning process. How he participates and the form of the Visual Bridges will depend on what skills he already has and what objectives he needs to work on. Visual Bridges can be adapted for both verbal and nonverbal students.

GOAL #3: provide more opportunities for the student to engage in communication and conversation about his experiences

The process of preparing and using Visual Bridges presents a built-in opportunity to rehearse and review significant information. It is an opportunity to:

- practice giving information
- build vocabulary
- share more details about personal experiences

Since this activity stresses expanding communication about the student's personal experiences, there is a high level of interest and a high rate of learning.

Once prepared, Visual Bridges are a tool to support both the student and his communication partner in a conversation about his experience. The visual symbols provide cues for both people so they know what to ask or what to tell.

Preparing Visual Bridges can become an integral part of school and home routines. Implemented at the student's level of comprehension and production, they develop into a valuable resource for improving communication. The most significant key for success is the degree of student involvement. The more the student participates, the more he will gain from this activity.

> *Preparing and using Visual Bridges gives students the opportunity to practice the oral and written vocabulary and language related to their life experiences.*

VISUAL BRIDGES

Visual bridges effectively support ongoing communication between home and school, the two primary environments for students. The same idea can be adapted for communication between other locations.

TODAY AT SCHOOL

Designed to guide the student in recounting what he did today, this activity can involve a summary of the whole day's activities or highlight some specific events. The idea is that the student reviews what occurred during the day and puts that information in a visual form to take home. If the student cannot recall from memory, he can go back to the schedule and use it as a guide to prepare his "Today at School". The specific format varies, depending on the educational level of the student. Activities include a range of levels such as:

- marking schedule pictures on a page of choices
- copying the names of activities from the schedule
- collecting food wrappers or advertising pictures from an excursion
- photocopying pictures or objects that communicate the information
- copying fill-in-the-blank sentences
- writing original sentences

TODAY AT SCHOOL

NAME _____

DATE _____

calendar time	aerobics	snack	workshop
seat work	leisure	cooking	music
lunch	VCR	computer time	community trip
	housekeeping	art	

The goal is active participation to prepare something to take home. The time spent reviewing and rehearsing will help the student remember and organize his thinking to prepare him for sharing that information as he carries it to the next environment. When the information is in a visual form, it serves as a tool for both the student and the other person to use for sharing. *The result is a sustained interaction where more information is shared.*

LAST NIGHT AT HOME

This system is particularly desirable for those students who love or desire "homework". This serves the same purpose as TODAY AT SCHOOL but in reverse. The goal is to share information in a visual form to encourage communication about the student's experiences outside of school. It is most difficult to teach language skills to students when you don't know the answers to the questions you ask. This format gives teachers more information to use when teaching communication. Here too, student participation is critical for maximum benefit from the activity. It is important for the student to have the responsibility for preparing the document in some way and in transporting it back to school. That process will encourage the student to initiate and participate in meaningful conversations.

name _____ date _____

LAST NIGHT AT HOME

For dinner I ate ___Hot dogs and jello___

On TV I watched ___Cartoons___

Our company was ___Grandma and Grandpa___

I played ___Legos___

We went ___to K mart___

I went to bed at ___9:00___

CREATING VISUAL BRIDGES

Developing visual bridges offers an opportunity to teach a wide variety of skills. Select a system that the student understands and can participate in. Effective visual bridges can be developed from any of the following formats or combinations of more than one.

Structured Picture Communication

Using the pictures that are used for the daily schedule, or pictures that relate to specific activities, the student assembles, marks, or in some form indicates what information is to be communicated. The student part might be:

■ photocopy the daily schedule

■ look at today's schedule and mark those pictures on a page of schedule pictures

■ cut and paste significant schedule pictures, labels, wrappers from treats, or anything the student will recognize

■ photocopy labels, boxes from foods or videos or other significant items

■ photograph something that is memorable

These activities work even for those students who have limited writing ability.

Dictated Language Experience

Language experience stories are created to encourage the students to retell events from their daily experiences or communicate important information. The student dictates thoughts that the teacher writes. A twist that is not as common is to support the written language activity with some form of pictures. Try using schedule pictures or hand drawn sketches. Even non-artists can draw enough for students to understand. The addition of the pictures can significantly improve the language recall and comprehension for students. It turns the activity from a "struggling reading" experience into an interactive communication exchange. Students who cannot accurately or reliably read the printed word may produce substantial language that is triggered by the picture portion of the message.

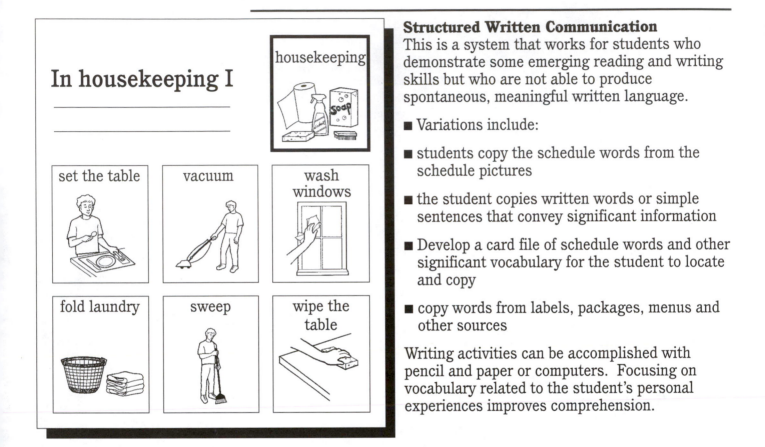

Structured Written Communication

This is a system that works for students who demonstrate some emerging reading and writing skills but who are not able to produce spontaneous, meaningful written language.

■ Variations include:

■ students copy the schedule words from the schedule pictures

■ the student copies written words or simple sentences that convey significant information

■ Develop a card file of schedule words and other significant vocabulary for the student to locate and copy

■ copy words from labels, packages, menus and other sources

Writing activities can be accomplished with pencil and paper or computers. Focusing on vocabulary related to the student's personal experiences improves comprehension.

Written Language Experiences

In this variation of the language experience activity, the student writes or types, rather than dictates, the information he wishes to share. The success of this form of language experience depends on his ability to produce written language. A variation of this is for the student to dictate and then copy what was dictated. Another option is to provide some pattern, fill-in-the-blank type sentences for the student to choose from. Try to create a personal dictionary or word bank to support the student's writing attempts. Including pictures in the student's writing can increase enthusiasm and clarify communication.

SAMPLES & EXAMPLES

> *REMEMBER: Although there are numerous ways to approach developing visual bridges, this is one system that has produced some remarkable results. The structure has helped many students with marginal reading and writing potential to develop some useful, functional literacy skills. Success has come from the simple organization of the system. It does not expect a lot of spontaneous language output from the students. The students are supported with the schedule and other classroom visual tools. Therefore, it is particularly effective with those who have limited expressive language and those who learn language in a more gestalt learning style.*

> *Visual Bridges can be developed to match the student's level of literacy. For many students, functional literacy and reading comprehension are increased because the activity evolves from their real life experience.*

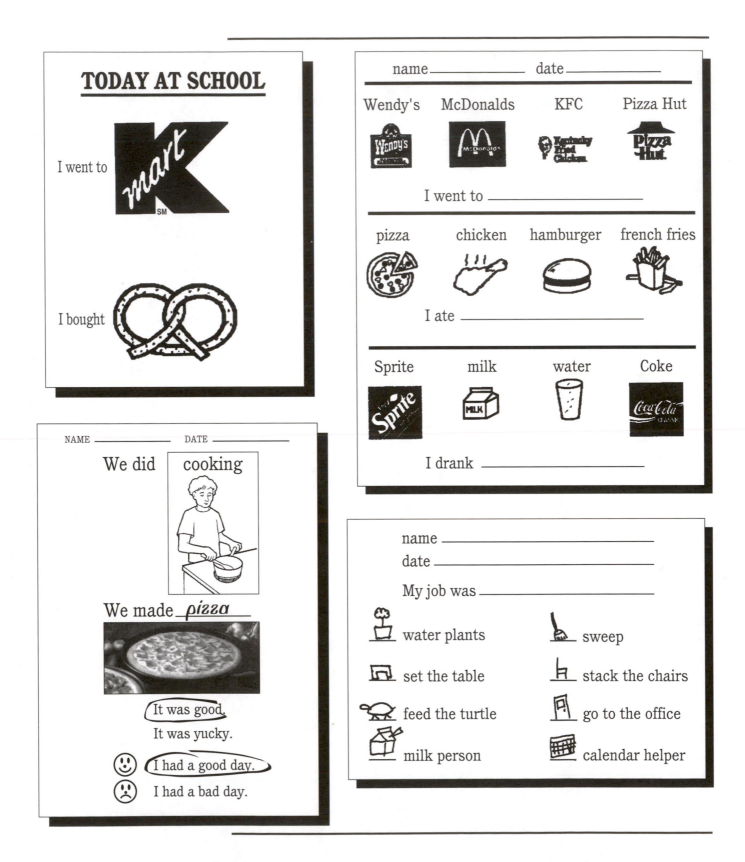

TODAY AT SCHOOL

I went to

I bought

---

name _____ date _____

Wendy's   McDonalds   KFC   Pizza Hut

I went to _____

pizza   chicken   hamburger   french fries

I ate _____

Sprite   milk   water   Coke

I drank _____

NAME _____ DATE _____

We did   cooking

We made *pizza*

It was good.
It was yucky.
I had a good day.
I had a bad day.

---

name _____
date _____
My job was _____

water plants   sweep

set the table   stack the chairs

feed the turtle   go to the office

milk person   calendar helper

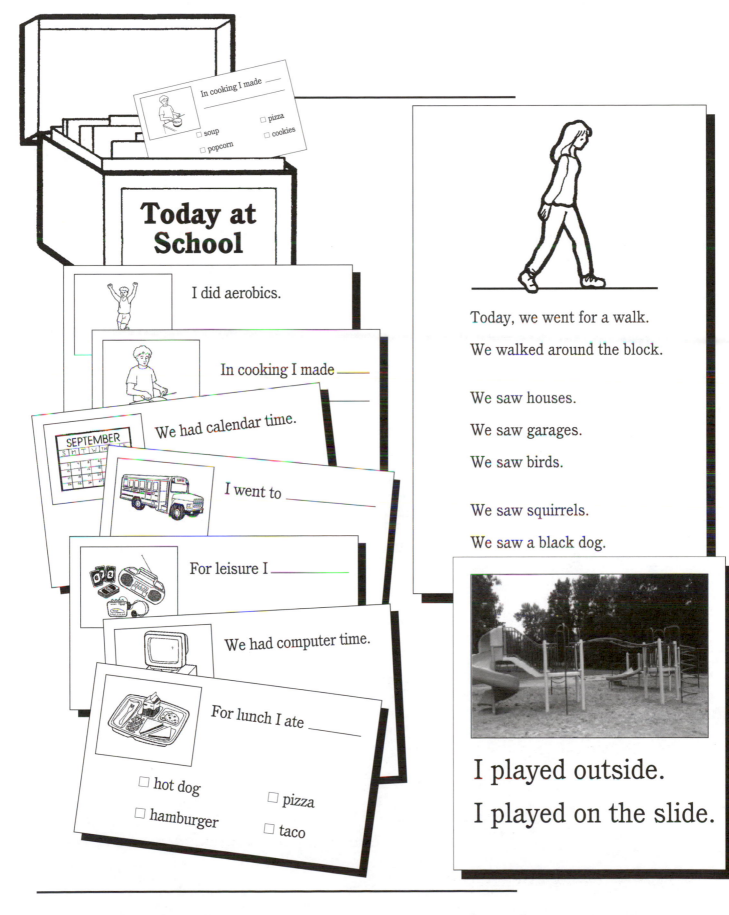

In cooking I made ——
☐ soup   ☐ pizza
☐ popcorn   ☐ cookies

Today at School

I did aerobics.

In cooking I made ——

We had calendar time.

SEPTEMBER
S M T W TH F

I went to ——

For leisure I ——

We had computer time.

For lunch I ate ——
☐ hot dog   ☐ pizza
☐ hamburger ☐ taco

Today, we went for a walk.

We walked around the block.

We saw houses.

We saw garages.

We saw birds.

We saw squirrels.

We saw a black dog.

I played outside.
I played on the slide.

SUGGESTIONS FOR BUILDING SCHOOL-HOME COMMUNICATION

Communication between school and home frequently becomes parents and teachers trying to write quick notes to each other. Turn school-home communication into an activity that is the student's responsibility. Teach the student to carry and share important information about his life. The result is functional communication training.

Using visual forms that the student recognizes easily encourages spontaneous sharing.

1. Use visual symbols that are easily recognized by the student
Their use is for the purpose of supporting interaction, not specific reading instruction. If created in a form that is too difficult for students to interpret, spontaneity will be reduced. The interaction will become distorted. It will lack a natural flow. Visual Bridges are tools to encourage and enhance communication exchanges, not replace the interaction. Improved student word recognition may come as a part of this process, but it is not the first goal.

2. Use words, picture/word combinations or other symbols that will be understandable to everyone who will be getting information from the communication tools
When a communication tool is crossing environments, it is essential that everyone involved be able to interpret clearly what is being represented. Label pictures so that there will be no misunderstanding.

3. Make the student as much a part of the preparation as possible
The more a student actively participates in this activity, the more he will take ownership of the product and the more he will learn. Many skills necessary to accomplish this information exchange fit with the student's other objectives (deciding what to share, dictation, discussion, typing, writing, using the photocopier, cutting, gluing, etc.). Sharing information between environments should be a student centered activity. It should not be turned into an elaborate communication project between the parent and the teacher. The goal is to give the student visual supports to assist in communicating the information he needs or wants to share.

4. Be flexible about *when* you include this activity in your day
It would not be logical to begin the day with a "what I did today" activity. Preparing home communications just before going home creates a perfect opportunity to review and summarize the day's activities. If enough time is not allotted, however, it can turn into a meaningless ritual to rush through before it is time to leave. Another option is to create a "TODAY AT SCHOOL" communication soon after a special activity, whenever it occurs in the day. That allows the opportunity to "capture the moment" and then rehearse and review that paper several times before it is sent home.

These activities can be inserted logically in the daily schedule to accomplish shorter or longer term memory goals to meet the child's needs.

5. Introduce the right amount of variety in your routines

Developing a routine for Today at School and Last Night at Home activities will encourage the student to anticipate the opportunity to share. The structure of the routine can help them become more complete in what they share. On the other hand, excessive mechanical routine encourages thoughtless, ritualistic responses that defeat the purpose of the activity. Redundancy will diminish the effect. Variations in type of activity or format keeps everyone interested. Thoughtful programming can include a combination of routines to encourage the functional independence and the variations to encourage the inclusion of new skills.

6. Use this medium to teach expanded communication

Communication, not perfect language structure, is the goal of these activities. Although this is a perfect opportunity to teach expanded language skills, focusing too much on language structure can inhibit the development of spontaneity. A tender balance is necessary. Attending to more pragmatic communication goals such as initiating conversation and taking turns may be more valuable.

7. Be a multimedia experimenter

Use lots of photos, catalog pictures, package labels, and other sources of visuals to enhance your visual supports. Have the students participate in finding and preparing them. Use originals or experiment with the photocopy machine, to reduce or enlarge items. If students can identify photocopies of objects or pictures, that expands the possibilities. Using these resources helps the student become more aware of finding objects in the environment to use to support giving information to others.

Use formats that are easily recognized by the student. That does not mean not to use writing. Include written words on the tools, even if the student is a non-reader or a limited skill reader. A combination of words and pictures teaches additional skills while preserving the student's rapid recognition.

REMEMBER: To derive the most from Visual Bridges it is essential for the people on both ends to understand the purpose. It is important to attempt to commit the time necessary for the student to engage in the communication that the tools will stimulate. It takes time to develop Visual Bridges. It takes time to participate in the communication that they generate. The rewards in student communication can far outweigh the time and effort devoted to the activity.

THE POINT IS: Visual tools created to mediate communication between environments can:

- give the student the responsibility of sharing information about himself

- reduce the amount of teacher-parent communication necessary

- teach the student to communicate more information effectively

- enable the student to share more information with more people

- enhance interpersonal interactions

- help communication partners better understand the messages that are shared

- make communication more rewarding and more enjoyable

Part 3

COMMUNICATING IN A VARIETY OF ENVIRONMENTS

Chapter 6

Improving Communication On The Homefront

Although the strategies presented in this book tend to focus on training in the school environment, it should never be forgotten that ultimately the purpose for training communication in school is to teach skills and discover systems that will make life outside school more successful for students. The same visual tools that provide support in the educational process will provide support in the student's home and family life.

Does that mean home and school should work together so we do everything exactly the same?

The use of visual tools to support communication transcends environments. Although general strategies are the same, there will be differences between home and school in implementation. For as much as we all preach establishing "consistency" between home and school, there are significant differences between the environments. School can become artificially structured, ignoring the human fluctuations that so frequently occur in the average home. On the other hand, students can experience a degree of freedom and self direction at home that cannot be permitted in school. Families and schools both establish routines based on the demands and needs unique to their environments. Considering this, *consistency becomes a similarity of style rather than a rigidity that cannot be modified.*

Are you suggesting everything at home should be visual?

A great wise man once said, "If it ain't broke...don't fix it." If there are parts of the home routine and communication interactions that work just fine, why change them? There is no reason to change things that already work just to make them "more sophisticated" or just so they match what happens in another place. As long as they accomplish the purpose adequately and everyone understands, why not spend the time and energy trying to improve a situation that is not working so well, or trying to change a situation that needs to be changed for a specific reason.

CONSIDER THIS SITUATION:

Andy and Dad have a great "get ready for bed" routine. The back and forth communication that they use and the routines that they follow are understood by both of them. It is a pleasurable activity. It works. No problem. Why change it? The problem occurs when Dad is not home for bedtime. Andy's routine doesn't work unless Dad is there. That is where the difficulty exists and that is where an intervention plan may suggest some visual aids to help Andy handle things without Dad. Why do the problems occur? Does Andy protest going to bed because Dad isn't there? Does he have difficulty transitioning to the different steps in the routine? The exact support strategies should be targeted toward solving the difficulties that occur when Dad is absent. Visual tools can give Andy the necessary information or guide him through a series of activities. It does not mean Dad and Andy need to change their routine, but Dad can develop some specific strategies to support Andy during his absences.

I tried to work with one family. We made some posters and pictures for home, but it didn't last long. Mom said she got tired of her house looking like school.

Communication supports need to meet the aesthetic and functional demands of the home. If family members are not comfortable with them, whatever the reason, the chances for their successful use diminishes to zero. They won't be used, or they won't accomplish their intended purpose. Original designs that work in other locations may need to be modified for successful integration into family life. Here is an example.

CONSIDER THIS SITUATION:

Jerry's mother worked with school staff to develop a set of pictures to keep in the kitchen to communicate about his food choices. Initially, Mom was enthusiastic about the pictures. They were hanging all over the kitchen. Jerry liked them, too. A follow-up investigation revealed that Mom had taken the pictures down and quit using them. She got tired of those pictures "hanging all over the kitchen." Evidently, their value for Jerry's communication was exceeded by Mom's desire for an uncluttered kitchen. Unfortunately, removing them was the only solution she entertained.

Both Jerry's communication needs and Mom's aesthetic tastes have to be considered when modifying the current system. It is possible to develop a format that will meet both requirements. For example, collecting the pictures to place in a box or photo album or putting them on the refrigerator instead of the cupboard doors are possible solutions.

HERE'S ANOTHER SITUATION:

Chad needed to learn to perform his bath routine more independently. Mom asked the teacher for help. Soon, their collaboration produced a carefully prepared 2'X3' poster board. It contained an excellent task analysis for independent bathing. Chad could read and understand the poster, so it was anticipated he would master this skill at home in a short time. The problem that surfaced was...where do you hang up a huge poster board in the normal family bathroom? Unfortunately, its lack of convenience undermined the project.

As well intended as these efforts were, the project didn't work. A few changes could have made a significant difference. Unfortunately, when a lot of effort has been expended for a disappointing result, people give up on future attempts to develop supports. Fortunately, keeping a few DO's and DON'TS in mind can make success more likely.

SIMPLE IDEAS FOR HOME

Using the visual strategies described in this book can support home communication in numerous ways. When presented with a lot of ideas, it can become a bit overwhelming to know where to begin. The best home systems and strategies are introduced a little piece at a time. Here are some ways to get started.

Use the refrigerator as a "communication center". Go to an office supply or craft type store and invest in:

- a package of magnets
    - *or*
- a strip of self-stick, adhesive backed magnet
    - *or*
- clear acrylic picture frames with magnet backs
    - *or*
- magnetic clips or hooks

Once you have the magnet capability, you will be surprised what you will find to hang up. Use the refrigerator to store visual tools to give your child information.

Create a family information center. Find a calendar with large squares. A desk size one will work great if you have a place to put it. Use it to give information about all family members. Include things like this:

- where people are going

- when they will come home late

- when they won't come home

- when regular events occur

- when special events will occur

- when company is coming

Invest in a little pocket size photo album. Something little to fit into a purse or pocket will be best for going away from home. Begin a collection of visuals to use to give your child information when you leave home. Include:

- places you are going

- choices to make

- rules to follow

- things to help changes or transitions

Begin a collection of valuable visuals. Keep a holder for visuals you find that you may need some day. Sometimes you find the right thing when you don't quite need it....a picture in a magazine or an advertisement, a menu from a favorite restaurant, a coupon for a certain store. Don't go crazy...just be efficient. Watch for "freebies". For example: Many restaurants have copies of their menus that you can take home. That would give you the opportunity to look at it with your child and plan ahead for dinner out.

Invest in a camera. See Chapter 9 for comments about cameras and taking pictures. The idea here is to capture what is real and meaningful for your child. Carry the camera in your car for a while. When you travel to some of the places that are significant to your child you can snap a picture to add to your files. Don't go running around town compulsively and wear yourself out. Just take a few during your normal routine. If it is an instant photo, have your child participate in taking it home to put in the photo album.

Use the pictures when you talk about what is going to happen. Take pictures of grandma & grandpa, friends or neighbors who are regularly in your life. Use them to tell your child what is going to happen. For example, use the picture of grandma & grandpa to tell your child they are coming over for dinner tonight. Then hang it on the refrigerator (with one of your magnets) and refer to it throughout the day in preparation

Use the household tools that surround you. Look around your home for those things already there that can be used to support communication: clocks, kitchen timers, TV guides, calendars, labels on packages. You probably already use some of these. When you focus on "visual" you may see opportunities you didn't think of before.

Help your child organize his space. Unclutter his personal space. Find a specific place for everything. Use boxes and holders to sort, organize, and categorize. Label spaces and drawers.

Organize other family member's space, too. Helping to differentiate what is yours from what is not yours will eliminate many opportunities for problems.

Give your child opportunities for activity. Have him participate in finding visuals, getting them out, putting them away and carrying them around. Have him hang things up, cross off things on the calendar or list and cut out the coupons.

Find things for your child to carry. Transitions are frequently difficult for kids. Giving them something to see and carry that relates to the destination can help. For example: try a coupon to be used at the grocery store, a shopping list for the mall, some clothing for the dry cleaners.

Assign specific places to keep visuals. If you buy that photo album and put a picture in it, but you can't find it when you need it, then frustration will overtake your efforts. Try places like the refrigerator, by the front door, in your purse in the glove box of the car, or in the specific room where you will use something.

Keep visuals in a place (or in places) that your child can access easily. Keeping them on top of the refrigerator where he can't reach them will defeat your purpose. Don't be surprised if your child develops an attachment to the visual tools. Sometimes parents report that taking them down and carrying them around becomes part of their child's routine. What will become important is to emphasize the communicative value of the visuals.

Keep visuals in the locations where you need them. Food items probably belong in the kitchen. Tools that you will use in the bathroom or bedroom can be kept in those rooms. It would not be convenient to run from the bedroom to get the picture from the kitchen to carry back to the bedroom. There may be some things you will decide to keep duplicates in more than one place.

Start with ONE thing. One picture or photo or label or sign is all you need to begin. It is good to have an idea of where you want to go, but start simple. After reading the suggestions in this book you may have identified several techniques that you think will work with your child. Still, start with one thing. Then build your plan one piece at a time. In six months or one year you will develop a collection of little things that will support communication at home. Plan on it taking that long. Go slowly. Just don't go so slow that you don't go anywhere.

USE the tools. Some people are "collectors" but not "doers". It is one thing to become involved (or over involved) in assembling visual tools. They won't have any value, however, unless they are used. It is important to collect and use your visuals gradually. That will help you know what is working best. That will prevent you from spending a lot of effort collecting things that won't work.

Teach your child how to use the visual tools. Just having them is not enough. Using them consistently when you communicate with your child is essential so he can learn their value.

Give your child responsibility. Have him participate as much as possible in the creation and use of the visual tools. Teach them to be responsible for getting things and putting them away when appropriate. After understanding the concept, it is not unusual for students to actively let you know what else to add to the collection. Listen. They will tell you what they want and need.

REMEMBER: Visual aids can enhance communication for the whole family, not just the child with special needs. Make it a family plan. Grasp the concept and be creative about how to adapt visual tools for your whole family.

DO'S AND DON'TS FOR SUCCESS AT HOME

Visual tools are intended to support communication anywhere that support is needed. There are numerous ways home can be enriched with these strategies. Here are some ideas to guide your thinking so your efforts will be productive.

PHILOSOPHY:

DO: Recognize that home and school are different. The needs are different and the demands in the environments are different.

DO: Remember that communication needs and communication goals may be different at home than at school.

DO: Remember that home may have many routines and interactions that work just fine and don't need to be changed.

DO: Recognize that the student may have skills to handle some interactions adequately at home, however, they may not be able to manage similar skills or situations away from home. There are other demands that he may handle fine in other locations but demonstrate difficulty at home.

DO: Remember that the solutions to difficulties may come in "lots of little pieces" rather than in one big dramatic change.

DO: Remember that visual strategies are not a "cure," but a collection of tools that can help if they are developed to meet your needs and then used.

DO: Recognize that communication interactions between communication partners need to be *efficient*. If given the choice between a more sophisticated-complex system and a simple-quick-easy system, most people will use what is easiest to produce the desired result.

DO: Make communication supports in a form that will be as universally understood as possible. This will encourage use by other family members, neighbors, baby sitters, relatives, etc.

PLANNING:

DO: Recognize that it does take time to plan ahead to create visual supports for the home, however, the time invested will produce positive changes in participation.

DO: Remember that students may need to be trained (retrained) to use visual tools in the home setting. Even if he uses a tool successfully at school or in another environment, generalizing to home may require extra help. Even though the same or similar tools are a part of the school routine, home is different.

DO: Develop visual supports one at a time.

DO: Keep in mind that developing a system of visual communication supports is an ongoing process. There should be continual changes...additions, deletions, modifications...as life evolves. If these changes do not accompany the changes in needs, the systems will not meet their potential.

DO: Know that you don't always have to go through a lengthy planning process. Come up with a simple, immediate solution for an immediate need.

PARTNERSHIP:

DO: Create a teacher-parent partnership for ideas for visual tools. This is a highly individualized craft. Making you own tools may produce results that target your needs more effectively than if you expect someone else to try to guess what will work for you. Everything for home and school does not have to be, and won't be, totally identical, but coordination helps.

DO: Recognize that all people in a partnership do not have to think exactly alike, either in perception of needs, or in finding a solution to those needs.

DO: Include the student as much as possible in the planning and preparation of visual tools for home use. You may be surprised what his input will tell you.

DO: Include other family members in the creation and use of the visual tools. When everyone understands the purpose of visual tools they will be more willing to participate in their use.

MAKE VISUAL COMMUNICATION A FAMILY AFFAIR:

DO: Remember that many visual aids will work for the whole family. For example, include all family members on a calendar or make visual versions of rules for all children.

DO: Consider using labeling systems, color coding and other organizational strategies for the whole family. Rather than think of visual communication supports as something that is "extra work" for one child, try to integrate these ideas into general family life. The more the child with special needs is a part of "how the whole family does it" the more effective the systems will be.

DO: Look for opportunities to use visual aids to support relationships with other people: baby-sitters, neighbors, visitors, etc. Explain to them what the tools are and their purpose in supporting your child. Once people understand, they will be more likely to enthusiastically participate.

FORMAT:

DO: Be aware of what formats will work best at home. Most families would be less enthusiastic about a huge poster board to hang on the wall than they would with something to hang on the fridge with magnets.

DO: Change things that do not work. The first try may not be perfect. Once you try to use something you will get ideas about how to make it more convenient or more effective.

DO: Be sure to write on the tools exactly what you say or do when using them so everyone will understand.

DO: Remember to include the visual aids that already naturally exist in your home. Everything does not have to be made special. The TV guide, wrappers and packaging from foods, coupons from your junk mail, and actual household objects can all be successful visual aids if used properly to support communication.

DO: Keep it simple. You are more likely to follow through to experience success.

Dear Parents:

Living with a child with special needs is both like and unlike raising other children. Raising any child is a process of learning and letting go. The techniques you use to manage your two year old prove ineffective by the time he is five or nine or sixteen. As the child grows and matures, his needs change. As the needs change, the parenting techniques get modified. In this way, all children present the same challenge to parents.

Parents grow weary. Keeping home and family balanced frequently involves more energy than they can sustain. The hope is that implementing visual strategies will make life easier at home for everyone. For this concept to really work, it is necessary to make it a dynamic process...things need to grow and change as life's demands present themselves.

Keep in mind that the concept of visual support does not mean only elaborately prepared tools. Techniques as simple as giving a child a newspaper coupon can communicate lots of information to guide a situation. Once the *visual* mind-set is established you will see lots of little things that will help. Putting intense pressure on yourself to produce an elaborate system may create more stress than it will solve. Conversely, putting some effort into tackling a few challenging situations may produce results well worth the time. The key is *lots of little things*. But *start with only one*. There is no formula for how much is the right amount. Only you will be able to answer that.

Wishing you a successful journey.

THE POINT IS: Visual tools are excellent resources for the home to:

- give information
- provide structure and organization
- manage behavior
- support communication and independent functioning for greater family enjoyment.

Chapter 7

Communicating In The Community

There is an increasing trend today to educate students with special needs to function as independently as possible in the community....the "real world." This educational direction brings with it many new barriers to go over, under, around, or through. Developing effective and efficient communication strategies to use for active participation in the community is probably one of the most challenging aspects of helping a student develop a functional *comprehensive* communication system.

There is surprisingly a great deal of diversity in philosophy regarding what forms of communication should be taught for community participation. Theories range from purist to practical. Regardless of the mind-set that one espouses, there are several factors that must be considered.

The first reality: Whatever works for a student in his school and home environments may fall very short in less familiar environments with less familiar people.

Understanding cues and information, giving information or making requests are some of the communication functions necessary for success in the community. Learning to interpret the environment is as critical as expression.

For purposes of this discussion, community will be defined as those places the student goes outside of his home or school environment. Community can include neighborhood, shopping, restaurants, homes of other people, church, doctor offices, travel, and all the other locations the student may visit.

The second reality: People in the community will vary considerably in their own communication abilities and in their tolerance for communication breakdown. No matter what skills the student possesses, there is a variable they cannot easily be prepared for.

The third reality: The community is unpredictable and unstructured; the opposite of a well planned educational environment or an orderly, routine home environment. There are so many variations for sharing information, getting instructions, and figuring out how to accomplish one's goals that even those without communication handicaps are frequently challenged. People with communication difficulties often face seemingly insurmountable obstacles.

The goals of educators and parents fill the spectrum from idealism to pessimism. The adult expectations for a student to function in the community may not reflect the student's real potential. Sometimes students are so protected that they are not given the opportunity for the independence they could achieve if they had some training and strategically developed supports. In contrast, when considerable effort has been put forth to adjust for students, people can see improvement, sometimes failing to recognize how much of that success is the result of their own adaptations and accommodations. This can produce a distorted expectation of student success in other settings. Getting a student ready for interaction in the community requires a very pragmatic approach.

The goal of this chapter is to provide a framework for considering the application of visual communication strategies to the student's existence outside of school and home. The purpose is not to provide an in depth discussion of augmentative communication. This discussion will not answer all the philosophical questions that arise about communication training. Instead, the focus will extend the discussion of visual supports to one more environment that is important to students. When thinking about them participating in the community, remember some basic observations that have been made in our discussion:

- Visual tools provide support for all parts of the communication circle: understanding, organizing, and expressing.

- Visual supports are a part of everyone's environment. We all use them.

- Sometimes the answers to big needs come in lots of little pieces.

- Any of the ideas in this book can be adapted to meet needs in the community.

ESTABLISHING GOALS FOR COMMUNITY PARTICIPATION

Considering the current social and educational trend to promote increased community participation for people who experience disabilities, the scope of this section will be to focus on those who have the potential for independent or monitored performance in the community. Although communication ability frequently determines how successfully students will accomplish their community goals, many who experience severe communication disorders can become highly successful in community environments with some training and support.

There seem to be many divergent philosophies about how to prepare students for functioning in the community.

Yes! One philosophy promotes the idea that the community should provide a lot of accommodation for people who experience special needs. The counter philosophy suggests those with special needs must learn compensations to enable them to access the community effectively. While society is battling this philosophy issue, it is imperative that we educate our students with a sensitivity that will prepare them to adequately function in the environments *they will live in.* To do this it will be necessary ask some questions.

What are the questions?

Although there are many, the following areas are critical to consider.

QUESTION 1: What are the family goals for the student?
This is a critical question. Otherwise time spent teaching a student may not be aiming toward the target. Where will he live? Where will he work? Who will he spend time with? Where will he go? What types of responsibilities will he have? The answers to these questions will begin to provide a foundation for targeting skills for individual students. There will be great variations of philosophies depending on the student's current age, ability level, family attitude, and the community where he lives. *It is important to remember, the answers may change over time as the family philosophy evolves, a student's age changes and his potential skill or lack of skill evolves.*

QUESTION 2: What is the student's current potential and realistic future potential in the community?

By teenage or adulthood, will he be able to manage in the community independently or with minor supports? Will he always need assistance or supervision? Does he exhibit appropriate community behaviors and understand community routines but just lack specific communication competency? Can he communicate adequately but needs support to handle the routines necessary to accomplish his goals? Is the communication breakdown just a part of a whole set of behaviors and skills the student needs to be taught? Identify your primary long term goal for the student in the community. Is it complicated, sophisticated communication or is it independence? Will his participation in the community reflect total independent functioning of all adult tasks and responsibilities, or will he learn how to participate in selected activities and routines? How tolerant is his community environment? How well known is he in the places he goes? Getting treats at the corner store on a regular basis is very different from attacking a shopping mall.

Wow! That is a lot of things to think about.

Yes, but it is important to consider the student's needs in a global way, with a long term vision. Otherwise, it would be easy to spend a lot of time teaching skills without targeting what he will really need. The even greater disaster is to send him out into life without equipping him with supports that could increase his participation and make his life a lot more satisfying. Students without handicaps learn skills in school that they generalize into other areas of their lives without specific training. Those with autism or other moderate to severe communication disorders often need training and support that is targeted to meet very specific needs. Of course, we want to do this in all educational areas, however the contact with community is a bit different.

Why is communicating in the community different from school or home?

The community is less flexible and less forgiving than more familiar places. The complex demands in the community, paired with its frequent lack of flexibility and accommodation, create a huge barrier to overcome. We generally have little control over modifying the community requirements, however, there are many ways we can employ visual strategies to accomplish some of life's routines. It is frequently difficult for all of us. That is why businesses have worked so hard to create "user friendly" systems and procedures. Since our identified students will take longer to learn, we need to target their needs to make the best use of their time.

OK. Now I need to put this in perspective of this visual concept. How does it fit in?

Remember that we are talking about the student's ability to successfully understand, organize himself, and express his intents to others. Understanding is enhanced by making use of the visual supports already present in the community. Although other students may do that without special training, many of the students we are talking about need to be specifically taught how to maximize the information and supports available to them. Personal organization is enhanced in many ways through visual strategies, regardless of the natural supports that are already available in the environment or by designing personal aids to meet identified needs.

What about students who talk? They don't need visual supports do they?

Remember, it doesn't matter if a student is verbal or nonverbal. Visual supports help them all *understand* better. In addition, speaking students can often be helped by using visual aids to help them express themselves. Consider these situations on a trip to the local restaurant:

- **The student whose articulation is not clear:** People who know him well may not have difficulty understanding him, but strangers don't always know what he is saying.

> *When the concept of functional reading or functional academics is brought up, some educators begin to list the "classics"; stop, go, caution. When was the last time you used those cues? Now think about the other visual information you use regularly: this lane open, sale, price tags, menus, cashier...Be sure you are targeting the most useful skills to teach, not just the ones that come in a neatly packaged kit to buy.*

■ **The student who has difficulty placing his order:** He can't remember what he wants or he forgets to order all the items.

■ **The student who can't remember or understand how to respond to the clerk's questions during the order process:** When he orders a hamburger, does he know what to do when the clerk asks, "Do you want the Bigger Burger or the Baby Burger?"

■ **The student who is not competent handling money:** He can't figure if he has enough money to buy what he wants, how much money to give to the cashier, or what size tip to leave.

All of these students could benefit from visual tools. Remember the many functions of those visual tools. They can give the structure necessary for selected tasks to be accomplished more easily and efficiently. Aids may not be the primary means of communicating, but they can be used to support the student by helping him organize his thoughts, be more concise, provide a forum for communication exchange or make the decisions necessary in a situation.

The more I think about it the more I realize how complex this can become. How can you develop visual aids for the community? Everything changes from location to location. You don't have the control that you do in more restricted environments. That is the problem, and that is why our assessment questions are so important. So much depends on the student's individual needs. You can't account for all the variables in the real world, but you can teach the student efficient routines and compensations. Some visual tools may be implemented as a life pattern: others may exist for a period of time as a training tool and then are eliminated when the student's needs change.

What types of visual strategies work?

We have only discovered the tip of the iceberg. Any of the concepts in this book can be adapted. The first step should be to teach students to use the supports that already exist for our use. Signs, menus, objects, and anything else that is available will work if the student knows how to interpret the information. After that, get creative. Remember, an underlying goal should be to aim toward independence.

Wow! I can tell there will be too much to teach!

Current state of the art educational practices suggest using the system of top down learning to teach students with special needs. This theory suggests that if students are trained to accomplish skills based on developmental norms, considering their learning rate, they may never get through the sequences. They may never learn all the steps and skills accomplished by students who do not have special needs. Consequently, their learning time will be used more efficiently if the end goals are targeted. Then the students can be taught the specific skills necessary to accomplish those targeted goals. This philosophy is compatible with the Outcomes Based Education that is currently defining special education planning.

> *Typical educational programs teach general skills and assume students will generalize those skills to their life environments.*
> *That may not happen for our students. The basic idea here is to be very specific in targeting what you want the goal to be. Then you can be sure to teach the skills and provide the supports necessary to reach that goal.*

OK, then where do we begin?

The Communication in the Community assessment will guide some observations of the student's skills and the environmental demands. That will define your direction. Then:

- Find out what the student wants to be able to do. That will show you where to begin.

- Target the types of activities the student presently participates in or would like to participate in.

- Identify what level of performance his peers would be accomplishing in those areas. That will establish the parameters for your decisions.

In keeping with the theme of this book, the purpose of this community assessment is to focus on identifying the communication components involved in accessing the community. Once you get a "mind set" of communication, you begin to realize how most tasks and actions have a communication component. Focusing on the communication demands in the situations will reveal many opportunities to help students achieve greater success through the use of visual supports.

ASSESSING PARTICIPATION IN THE COMMUNITY

More and more educational programs are extending training to community environments. Observing the student handling interactions and transactions in the community will yield more information than assuming how he would manage. Training in the community environment will also produce better results than simulating the experiences.

Although observations will produce an abundance of information, four main questions should structure your assessment.

1. Is the student's current performance **effective**? Does the student accomplish what he is trying to accomplish, clearly and purposefully, without extraordinary difficulty? Does his behavior reflect understanding of the demands of the environment?

2. Is the current performance **efficient**? Are the tasks accomplished easily with a minimum of frustration or confusion?

3. Are the current methods of accomplishing student goals **easy to use**? Does *everybody* involved understand what they need to understand?

4. Does the current system reflect **appropriateness** for the community? Does it encourage and allow the community to participate easily? Does it respect time constraints frequently necessary in public settings?

5. Is the training aiming toward **more independent** performance of the goals?

The assessment titled COMMUNICATION IN THE COMMUNITY will guide your observations as you identify specific community activities to evaluate; assess the environment, identify specific communication skills necessary to successfully participate in that environment, and evaluate the student's performance in that activity. The answers to these questions will form a framework from which you can make decisions about *1*. what skills to teach, *2*. what environmental supports already exist for the student to access, and *3*. where visual tools would provide extra help to increase independence.

COMMUNICATION IN THE COMMUNITY

Name_____ Date_____

Birthdate / Age_____ Evaluator_____

THE SITUATION

What activity will the student participate in?

❑ dine   ❑ shop   ❑ other:_____

❑ errand   ❑ appointment   _____

❑ work   ❑ recreation   _____

Will the student be accompanied OR unaccompanied?

Will the student be in an environment that is familiar OR unfamiliar?

Goals to be accomplished:

❑ eat

❑ work

❑ participate in leisure activity

❑ make a purchase

❑ make return (bottle return, return a purchase, etc.)

❑ request information

❑ accomplish specific business (bank deposit, pay bill, doctor appointment, etc.)

❑ other: _____

Skills necessary to accomplish the goals:

Type of location:

- ❑ small, free standing business
- ❑ office building
- ❑ large environment, i.e., shopping mall
- ❑ other: _____

- ❑ church
- ❑ doctor office
- ❑ public entertainment

Specific needs:

- ❑ find desired location
- ❑ know where to enter / exit
- ❑ other: _____

- ❑ make selections
- ❑ follow rules/procedures
- ❑ find restrooms

What environmental barriers need to be accessed:

- ❑ doors that open special ways
- ❑ following signs, arrows
- ❑ standing in lines

locating:
- ❑ elevators
- ❑ aisles
- ❑ other: _____

- ❑ escalators
- ❑ specific counter

- ❑ room numbers

Rules or routines necessary for success in this environment.

What helps or supports are already available in the environment?

What prompting or assistance is available in the environment?

people:
- ❑ secretary
- ❑ courtesy desk

- ❑ special helpers
- ❑ security guards

- ❑ clerks / cashiers

written:
- ❑ instructions
- ❑ directories
- ❑ signs

Specific communication demands in the situation:

UNDERSTANDING:

VERBAL COMMUNICATION:
- ❏ listen for name /number / turn
- ❏ understand requests, questions
- ❏ understand information or explanations given or conversation of others

NONVERBAL COMMUNICATION:
- ❏ gestures
- ❏ body language
- ❏ facial expressions

READING OR INTERPRETING:
- ❏ signs
- ❏ menus
- ❏ addresses / room numbers
- ❏ charts / lists / name plates
- ❏ directions to follow procedures
- ❏ directions to operate machines
- ❏ identify specific items / products / brands
- ❏ recognize labels / sizes / kinds / colors / flavors
- ❏ identify prices
- ❏ identify who is the correct person (ie. the cashier, salesperson, security person)
- ❏ correct change only / machines take only specific coins
- ❏ shopping list

EXPRESSION:

EXPRESSIVE COMMUNICATION:
- ❏ make requests / protests
- ❏ give information / answer questions
- ❏ social conversation

WRITING:
- ❏ sign name
- ❏ fill out form
- ❏ mark boxes, keep score

What is the student's present level of performance in the community locations identified?

How do other students of the same age handle this environment? What is their level of participation?

How is the student able to make use of the supports and assistance that are available?

Where do the breakdowns occur?

What currently happens when breakdowns occur?

What additional skills does the student need to learn?

What environmental supports does the student need to learn to access?

What visual supports could be developed to help the student prepare, organize, and follow through with the goals?

What training or supports would help the student accomplish his purposes and become:
- ❑ more effective
- ❑ more efficient
- ❑ more appropriate for the community
- ❑ more independent

What level of participation is expected by the time this student leaves school?
- ❑ independent
- ❑ independent with supports
- ❑ partial participation
- ❑ supported

CREATING SUCCESS IN THE COMMUNITY

Visual strategies can provide support for students as they participate in the community settings they visit. Just as students perform better in school and home environments that are enriched with visual supports, they can benefit from assistance in the community.

Considering the ideas presented in this book, what is the best communication system for students going out into the community?

There is no one right technique. There is no simple formula. The answer will probably evolve as lots of little pieces. Assessing the individual needs in the places a student visits will produce the answers. Here are some things *TO DO* while engaging in that process.

DO: Thoroughly assess the skills needed to function in the environment

The results of a thorough task analysis usually surprises people. Conducting a simple transaction in the community generally requires many more steps and more communication elements than we realize.

DO: Target the essential skills for success

Identify what parts the student can already handle adequately. Remember, there is a wide range of acceptable action in the community. The goal will be success, not perfection.

DO: Focus on teaching the routines the student needs to learn to accomplish his goal

Current learning theory suggests teaching the whole routine as a chunk rather than teaching isolated skills and expecting the student to assimilate them into a whole. When participating in the whole routine, the context will provide imbedded cues to give added support.

DO: Train students to get information from supports that already exist in the natural environment

The environment is filled with signs, objects, menus, and assorted other useful tools if a student knows what to do with them. Read the menu to get information. Match the pictures on the coupons with the items on the shelves. Scan the choices available. Locate, read and follow the signs and directions that direct the desired flow of activity. Many students do not adequately access the information that is already available for them. Looking, gesturing or pointing to draw attention to mutual referents is a skill that will help students get more information.

DO: Teach students how to point to or refer to things in the environment to support their communication attempts
Gesturing to or pointing to mutual referents can help the listener understand more quickly what is being communicated. Use the menu as a natural communication board by pointing to the items desired. Point to a sign to indicate a request. Teaching students to enhance their communication attempts by focusing on mutual referents will encourage the listener to use those referents also. This enhances the efficiency of the interaction.

DO: Strive for simplicity
Will a simple cue card to be pulled out of a pocket or wallet get the job done just as well as larger or bulkier options? Is a form filled out ahead, or a sample prepared to copy easier than taking the valuable time necessary to memorize information? Using a separate tool for each location or transaction may make interactions easier than attempting to include everything on one massive tool.

> *Remember, even verbal students may need support to organize their thinking or to help repair communication breakdowns.*

DO: Consider training students to use augmentative aids as supports for back and forth communication exchange with the other person
If set up properly, tools can support both understanding and expression for the student and the community. Students can be trained to handle and position the tools in ways to encourage other people to use them, too.

DO: Remember the student may experience difficulty understanding what is requested of him
Structure the use of the visual tools to bridge that gap. Many communication partners will naturally point to the tools to assist the communication process if the aids are simple enough and self explanatory enough for immediate comprehension.

DO: Design tools in sizes that are convenient to use
Those that fit in a pocket, purse or wallet are most easy to carry. In spite of the goal of convenient size, written words and picture symbols need to be large enough to be identified quickly.

DO: Design tools using symbols that are universally understood
Non familiar people should be able to immediately recognize what idea or information is being represented. Using written words with pictures helps clarify their intents.

DO: Recognize that a student's needs or desires may be very predictable

Simplify communication aids to accommodate for that. If he places the same order every time he goes to his favorite fast food restaurant, perhaps he needs only those items on his communication tool. If he follows the same routine or needs the same assistance consistently, the tool should specifically target his need. Don't make it more complicated. Attempting to allow for all the possible options makes communication situations too complicated.

DO: Prepare before going into the community

Making preparations ahead of time can help save time at the point of performance. Tasks such as reading the menu ahead of time, preparing orders, making sure students have money in a form they can be successful with, or creating shopping lists can make the community excursion more educational and more successful. Anticipate specific communication needs and prepare for them.

DO: Teach students ways to physically manage visual supports so they will be effective

Think about where to put them and how to hold them. When using a tool to support communication to another person, emphasize pointing with a coordinated, accurate point. Stress holding items so others can see them clearly. Students need to learn to pay attention to determine if they have their listener's attention.

DO: Teach students to be responsible for their personal tools

Remember to take the visual supports when departing for the community. Remember to use them at the appropriate time during a transaction or interaction. Remember to put them away for the next use. Taking care of the tools is an important part of the routine.

DO: Be considerate of the time constraints in the environment

If you are in a fast food restaurant during the lunch hour rush, an ordering system that takes a lot of time is not appropriate. Students need to be able to accomplish their transactions in a way that does not place inappropriate demands on others. In situations where the time element is not critical, more elaborate options may be appropriate.

> *Remember, visual supports can provide help for both the student and the people in the community.*

> *Many current clothing styles do not have pockets, or the pockets are too small for comfortable use. Try a fanny pack. They can be functional for both boys and girls. Then students can become responsible for their own personal visual tools.*

DO: Be sensitive to the public's ability to interpret student communication attempts

All people in the community do not understand or communicate equally. Even though a student can understand you, he may not understand people in the community. Even though you can understand a student's speech and communication attempts, the public may have difficulty. People can become embarrassed when a communication breakdown occurs. Try to avoid that kind of situation. Teaching students to use alternate strategies when communication breakdowns occur will make interactions more successful. Striving for universally understood communication strategies will ensure greater success.

DO: Structure the communication exchanges to be as easy as possible to achieve success

Even though students may be able to handle more complicated skills at home or school, the demands in the community are different. They may demonstrate a preference for a system that is less sophisticated or less complicated because it is more comfortable for them to use.

DO: Develop systems that help students look as normal as possible

Even though technology is increasingly easy to access, lugging a brief case sized computer to a convenience store may not be as convenient or effective as using a small card that fits in a wallet.

DO: Keep student preferences in mind

They will have greater success with something they like and feel comfortable with. Visual supports can be created in infinite varieties of sizes and shapes to meet the demands of student needs and desires.

DO: Aim for independence

If a student can do a really complicated transaction with the help of another person but he can't do it without the person, then it is too hard. Move back to a simpler format that the student can handle independently.

These suggestions are not all inclusive: The purpose is to encourage you to think globally. Often, little things determine if a student handles the environment independently, looks capable, or experiences frustration. Don't be deceived by a student's apparent intelligence....find out where the breakdowns are. Don't be surprised to find a college level computer student who can't effectively buy a snack in a convenience store. Similarly, some students with comparatively limited communication abilities handle community transactions more independently than we anticipate. A broad definition of communication encourages us to focus on observing the range of skills necessary to participate effectively in other environments.

Some educational settings allow more access to community environments for training purposes than others do. Regardless of your access, an awareness of student community functioning can help formulate educational objectives which will teach skills that will apply to this area of a student's life.

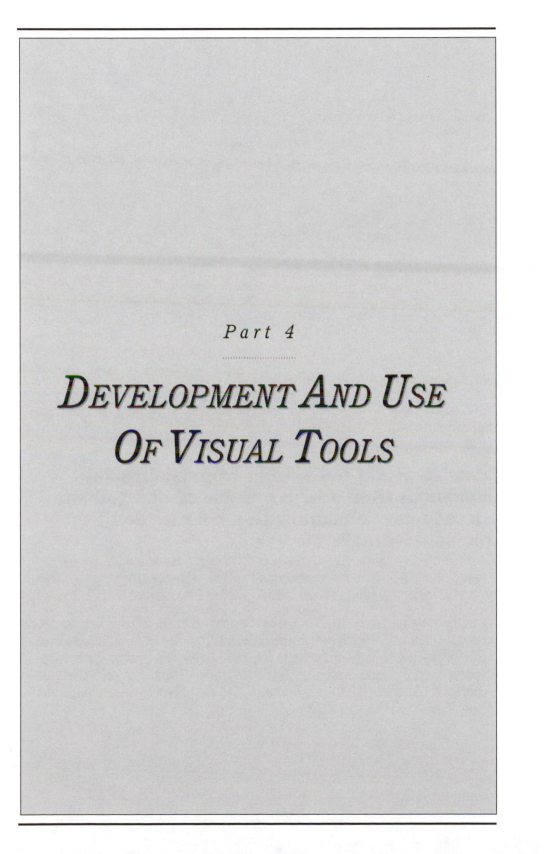

Part 4

DEVELOPMENT AND USE OF VISUAL TOOLS

Chapter 8

Developing Visual Tools

The differences between traditional communication boards and other visual communication tools does not make them mutually exclusive. Rather, exploring the differences can broaden the thinking about how they can be used and the functions for which they can be useful. The challenge of using visual communication tools is to creatively discover more functional and useful applications for them.

Anyone in the field of education is experienced with the "cut and paste" approach to educational supplies. Developing visual tools is not unlike your other experiences.

How do visual tools differ from traditional communication boards? Some of my students already use communication boards. Isn't this the same thing?

This book is not focusing on the development of the same kind of communication boards that have been designed for those students. In fact, using the name "communication board" risks a misunderstanding.

Communication boards for the physically impaired are created with a number of constraints and objectives that are different from the needs and objectives of other populations. The commonalty is: Both systems use visual symbols of some type as a means to mediate communication. Other than that, the differences far outweigh the similarities. (See Augmentative Communication Chart, Page 145).

Augmentative Communication:

Traditional Communication Boards	Visual Communication Tools
GOAL:	**GOAL:**
■ augment or support student's expressive communication to others	■ improve comprehension of communication ■ improve understanding of environment ■ increase attending and auditory comprehension skills ■ support organization and processing of communication and information ■ enhance communicative intent and interaction skills ■ teach skills ■ teach self regulation ■ develop more effective expressive communication ■ increase independent performance
Primary impairment: physical handicap, non verbal or ineffective verbal communication	Primary impairment: difficulties with communication, attention, organization, memory, communication interaction, word retrieval, comprehension of verbal communication, expressive communication and more
WHO USES IT:	**WHO USES IT:**
■ students who are non verbal or who have limited intelligibility	■ used by both the student and those people he is engaging in communication interactions with ■ teachers: to support communication *to* students ■ students: to *understand* communication, regulate behavior, learn tasks, and other functions

Traditional Communication Boards	Visual Communication Tools
PURPOSE:	**PURPOSE:**
■ used primarily as the student's expressive mode of communication	■ establish student attention
■ used primarily for the purpose of student expressing communicative functions such as requesting, protesting, and informing	■ a tool to give information to the student
■ assumes the student has a functional level of cognition and auditory comprehension for communication	■ used as cues and prompts for giving directions to students, training skills, and teaching sequence
■ may be student's major reliable communication form	■ a means to teach organization and relationships
	■ increase communication interaction skills
	■ recognizes students may benefit from support for effective communication whether or not they are verbal
	■ a support for communicating many expressive functions such as: requesting, protesting, and informing
	■ one part of a well developed communication system
PHYSICAL APPEARANCE:	**PHYSICAL APPEARANCE:**
■ frequently high tech, may be low tech	■ generally low tech
■ may need many symbols to be placed in a limited amount of physical space to enable student to access them	■ no physical space limitations since most students have sufficient motor coordination to turn pages and move materials from one location to another
■ a goal is to include the student's whole communication repertoire in as compact a space as possible	■ frequently work best when there are obvious categorical separations of symbols to help students associate with specific activities or locations
	■ frequently more efficient and effective when separate aids are created for separate functions or activities

Traditional Communication Boards	Visual Communication Tools
LOCATION OF USE:	**LOCATION OF USE:**
■ may require symbols to be placed in a limited range or distance from student ■ portability for mobile students requires something student can carry with him at all times	■ many need to be portable so they can be carried to various locations ■ can be displayed permanently on walls, desks, doors, etc. ■ work best when located strategically in the environment where they will be used ■ need to be located at the center of activity ■ need to be easily accessible to all users
SPECIFIC APPEARANCE:	**SPECIFIC APPEARANCE:**
■ student may be limited in mobility so aids that require movement, page changing or physical selection are dependent on assistance from another person ■ aids for mobile students generally scaled to be small to fit in a pocket or similar portable system ■ assume a level of cognitive understanding so they may use abstract symbol systems	■ can be assembled in variety of individual signs, charts, books, and holders to promote convenient use ■ can utilize physical movement as part of the use: turn pages, select choices, put selections in a holder, take things out or turn them over, etc. ■ size is determined by need...can range from a small piece of paper to a large poster or bulletin board ■ recommend very concrete, universally understood symbols for student understanding and universal comprehension by the wide variety of people who will access it ■ most effective aids use combination of picture and written words to describe or label the action or object represented
LINGUISTIC STRUCTURE:	**LINGUISTIC STRUCTURE:**
■ goal frequently involves development of language structure, ie. the assimilation of nouns, verbs, etc., to generate sentences ■ symbols frequently organized in a linguistic manner so students can select nouns, verbs, and other word categories to generate unique sentence construction	■ emphasis on communicating concepts rather than developing specific language structures ■ recommend one symbol for one broad concept or idea ■ supports the use of more limited language structures with effective communication as the primary goal ■ does not emphasize using or developing whole sentences ■ limited number of steps required for expressing an idea and receiving a response so communicative intent isn't lost

Traditional Communication Boards	Visual Communication Tools
AUDIENCE: ■ may be primarily limited to familiar others due to limited access to a broader community ■ speed of interaction important, but environment may be tolerant of special needs of student	**AUDIENCE:** ■ broad audience includes staff, peers, family, general community ■ speed of interaction important to maintain natural communication flow
VOICE OUTPUT: ■ sometimes desirable as a means to get attention or clarify communication ■ often considered an important element for maintaining interest and interaction	**VOICE OUTPUT:** ■ generally not necessary since purpose is to support communicative intent and interaction ■ students learn other means to get attention
HOW USED: ■ generally, student uses aid to respond, comment or question while his communication partner communicates verbally ■ overlays may need to be changed by communication partner	**HOW USED:** **in interaction:** ■ used as a receptive and expressive mode for both student and communication partner ■ speaker should point, hold or move tool to capture attention of listener ■ communicate message simultaneously with visual tool and any other forms (ie., speech or gestures) the person is able to use **for self-regulation:** ■ student should learn responsibility for accessing tools as needed, manipulating them in use, and caring for their location and following their procedures **for instruction:** ■ to teach skills or modify behavior ■ to give information

TEACHER TOOLS

One of the major differences between traditional communication boards and other visual tools is that of ownership. Frequently the tools belong to the teacher. They are Teacher Tools.

What are Teacher Communication Tools?

Most people think the primary purpose of augmentive communication is assisting students to communicate to others. **TEACHER COMMUNICATION TOOLS** provide a different focus. They are the *teacher's* instruments to communicate *to* the student. Think of the communication tools as an extension of the teacher's voice. The *goal is to provide simultaneous verbal and visual input* to the students when giving directions, asking questions, and other interactions.

Most of the visual tools in this book can be developed for the purpose of becoming Teacher Communication Tools. Teacher Tools serve many useful functions to enhance communication exchanges.

1. The teacher models a form of simultaneous communication-pairing verbalization with pointing to visual stimuli, pictures and / or word combinations.

2. Teacher Tools can be used to support communication to both verbal and non verbal students. The tools are used primarily to provide support to help the students attend and understand.

3. The tools enable the teacher to *reduce* verbalization which improves comprehension for many students.

4. Visual tools require some forethought and planning. The advantage is they guide staff to become more specific about what is being communicated and they encourage consistency among teachers, support staff, and others who are a part of interactions.

5. They help teachers be more consistent about expectations, procedures, and routines.

6. Students attend better. They focus their attention and demonstrate better understanding, retention and follow through.

7. Student behavior is improved across settings and with a variety of people when the communication tools provide consistency.

Is the teacher the only person who uses these teacher tools?

The concept of the teacher book can be expanded for use by others who are in a position of instructing or interacting with the student. Most programs are staffed with a variety of people (aides, therapists, secretaries, lunch ladies, principals, etc.) who have cause to direct students and communicate with them. As the teacher develops a functional set of teacher tools, it will be important for the significant others in the student's life to use those same successful tools to enhance their own interactions with him. Logistics may help determine how that can be accomplished. An aide who works closely with the teacher in the same room all the time may experience success using the same tools that the teacher does. If they are frequently working in different locations in the classroom or different rooms, the aide may need her own tools...perhaps a duplicate of the teacher's. A lunch lady who monitors the lunch room for students from several classrooms may have a communication page developed specifically for her job and location. The coordination of systems from class to class and student to student is important so there is some semblance of universality and continuity among them.

REMEMBER: Teacher tools have value for students with a wide range of abilities. Higher skilled students benefit from the use of visual tools to help them focus their attention and organize their thoughts. Students with more severe communication difficulties respond even better than when presented with only verbal interactions. *It does not matter whether a student is verbal or non verbal.* It does not matter what forms he uses for his own expressive communication. The teacher tools are used to mediate communication interactions between students and others, but the primary purpose for the teacher tools is to communicate *to* the student.

Who else will these tools work for?

The current trend to include students with special needs into regular education classrooms creates the need for some creative strategies to assist these students toward independent functioning in a large group setting. Rather than single out the student with special needs, classrooms are enhanced by building visual supports for the whole class.

SAMPLES & EXAMPLES

PROBLEM: The teacher needs to talk to and direct students in a variety of environments throughout the day. Inevitably the visual tool she needs to use is in another room or lost under a pile of papers on a desk somewhere.

SOLUTION #1: Make duplicates of specific visual tools and leave them in the location where they will be used. If the same communication page is used in the bathroom and when getting off the bus, make two copies and keep one permanently in the bathroom and the other where you can get it while going to the bus.

SOLUTION #2: Create a "teacher book". That is a notebook with the pages and communication tools that the teacher needs all in one location. A teacher book can be any size or shape, however, a larger 3-ring binder size notebook proves most successful for many because it is so big that it is harder to lose. Since the tools are all in one holder it is easy for the teacher to carry it around to various parts of the classroom or to various locations in and out of the building. The goal is to build a habit of that book always being within an arm's reach. It is the *teacher's* communication device.

The teacher book can contain the daily schedule, pages of rules, directions, pages to enhance communication during specific events or activities, or those comments / questions / corrections that the teacher uses frequently with her students.

> *Educators are very creative people when it comes to adapting ideas they glean from other sources. Frequently, that produces interesting and creative results. The shortcoming is when that adaptation process limits our scope of possibilities for a different population.*

PROBLEM: The student lives in a group home type setting where there is rotating supervisory staff. Because all the staff is not there at the same time and they have little opportunity to coordinate their programming, there is a great deal of variation in how they relate to residents and what kind of directions they give.

SOLUTION: Develop a set of staff communication tools. Make sure that instructions about how to use them are an obvious part of each tool to enhance consistency. This can be particularly helpful for new staff or substitutes.

THE POINT IS: Teacher communication tools are used to enhance communication *to* the student. They are a part of the *teacher's expressive* mode and the *student's receptive* mode. They help make communicating to the student:

- more effective
- more efficient
- more consistent
- more reliable
- more enjoyable

HOW TO MAKE VISUAL TOOLS

The development of visual tools can be a highly personal and creative process. The exact way people approach this project will reflect their personal style, organizational approach and artistic expression. Although it would be more convenient if teachers could just buy ready-made products, most visual tools require a degree of individualization for the particular person or situation. Personalization for a person or location is one of the most important elements for a successful result.

The purpose of this chapter is to provide some of the "nuts & bolts" of developing visual tools. The GUIDE FOR PLANNING COMMUNICATION TOOLS will provide some structure for your thinking. The rest of the chapter shares concrete "how-to" information.

Team up with others when going through the development process. This is a perfect time to develop a collaborative relationship between teachers and others who have input in the student's educational program. Talking through the questions on the GUIDE FOR PLANNING COMMUNICATION TOOLS with another person who is familiar with the student's daily performance will provide a forum for confirming observations and checking the clarity and reasonableness of proposed visual tools.

Once people decide to use some visual communication tools as a part of student programming, there is a tendency to want to implement many ideas. There is a temptation to push to get them done and in use as quickly as possible. The wisest advice is: *Don't move too quickly. This is a long term project.* The biggest mistake you can make is to embrace the idea of Visually Mediated Communication, think of 22 things to do and then go photocopy 4000 pictures. It won't work. Start with one idea and develop one piece at a time. Then you will achieve success. Remember, someone with a lot of wisdom once said, a successful journey begins with a single step.

> *Warning: The development of Visual Communication Tools can be somewhat time consuming if you do it right! Don't be in too much of a hurry. The planning stage is the most important. If traversed too quickly you may end up using a lot of effort to create a product that will, at worst, not accomplish your purposes, or at best, be much less effective than what you could have created. Once they are set up, the tools will save you lots of time and energy on a daily basis, making that original effort very worthwhile.*

GUIDE FOR PLANNING COMMUNICATION TOOLS

Student _____ Date_____

Birthdate / age: _____ Evaluators _____

EVALUATING THE SITUATION

The Environment

What is the Location:

Who is present:

Who is in charge:

What is the ongoing activity:

What routine is expected:

What student participation is expected:

What student behavior is expected:

What actually occurs:

What is the actual student performance or participation:

How is the situation managed:

How do current directions or interventions work:

What communication supports are currently being used:

What changes need to occur:

Environmental modifications:

Student performance:

What communication needs are observed:

What environmental supports could help:

What communication interactions need support:

What situations / behaviors need improvement:

The Student

 how does the student presently handle the environment:

 how does the student manage specific tasks or routines:

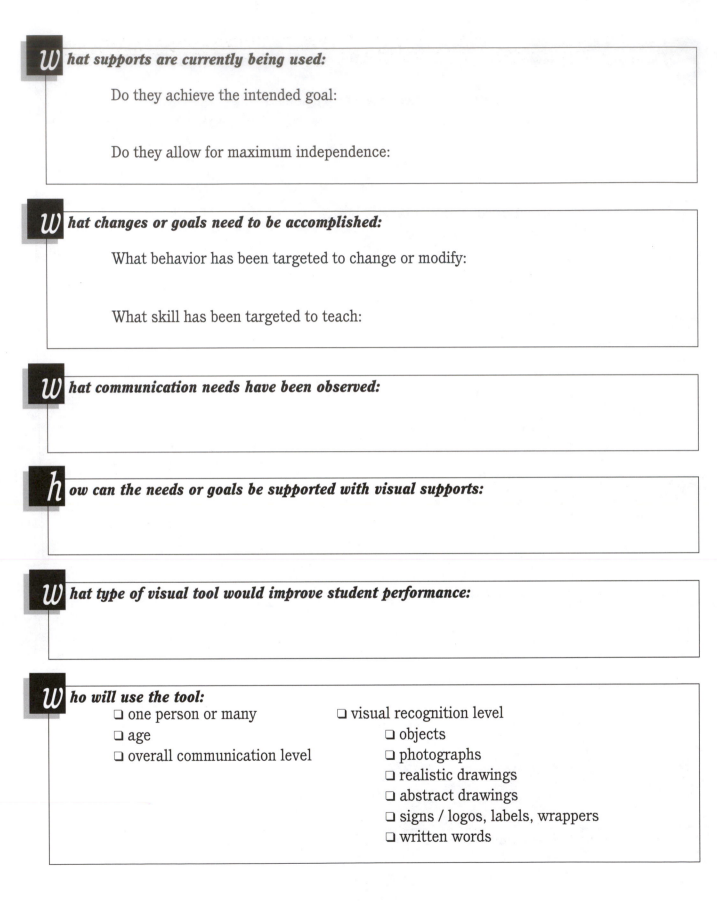

What supports are currently being used:

Do they achieve the intended goal:

Do they allow for maximum independence:

What changes or goals need to be accomplished:

What behavior has been targeted to change or modify:

What skill has been targeted to teach:

What communication needs have been observed:

how can the needs or goals be supported with visual supports:

What type of visual tool would improve student performance:

Who will use the tool:
- ❑ one person or many
- ❑ age
- ❑ overall communication level
- ❑ visual recognition level
  - ❑ objects
  - ❑ photographs
  - ❑ realistic drawings
  - ❑ abstract drawings
  - ❑ signs / logos, labels, wrappers
  - ❑ written words

PLANNING VISUAL TOOLS

W *ho will the tool belong to:*
- ❏ the teacher
- ❏ the student
- ❏ both teacher and student
- ❏ the whole class

W *here will the visual tool be used:*
- ❏ in a specific location
- ❏ in several locations
- ❏ during transition between locations

W *hen will the tool be used:*
- ❏ through the day as the need arises
- ❏ for a specific situation or activity
  - ❏ school
  - ❏ home
  - ❏ community

h *ow will it be used:*
- ❏ giving directions
- ❏ giving information
- ❏ asking questions
- ❏ encouraging independent performance
- ❏ handling a specific need
- ❏ managing a specific problem
- ❏ mediating communication between people
- ❏ mediating communication between environments
- ❏ teaching new skills or tasks

W *hat form of symbols will be used:*
- ❏ written words
- ❏ pictures
  - ❏ line drawings
  - ❏ detailed drawings
  - ❏ black and white
  - ❏ colored
  - ❏ size _____
- ❏ photographs
  - ❏ size _____
- ❏ actual labels & wrappers, signs logos
- ❏ cut outs form magazines, coupons, etc.
- ❏ objects
- ❏ a combination

W **hat will the aid look like:**
- ❏ size
- ❏ shape
- ❏ color

W **hat form will it be:**
- ❏ card
- ❏ paper
- ❏ chart
- ❏ book

h **ow will it be used:**
- ❏ who will use it for understanding
- ❏ who will use it to support expression

W **hat will be said when using the aid:**
- ❏ what is the exact "script" or vocabulary _____
- ❏ how will the aid be labeled so everyone using it will know what it says

h **ow will it be manipulated:**
- ❏ take a person to the aid
- ❏ take the aid to a person
- ❏ point to it
- ❏ hand it to someone
- ❏ turn pages
- ❏ put the pieces in a specific location
- ❏ cross something off
- ❏ cover something up

W **ill it be transported:**
- ❏ keep it in one location
- ❏ move it around to various locations

W **ho will move it:**
- ❏ teacher
- ❏ student

W here will the aid be kept:
- ❏ hanging on a wall
- ❏ on a door
- ❏ on a board or cabinet
- ❏ on table or desk
- ❏ in a container
- ❏ in a pocket
- ❏ in a communication book or location or holder
- ❏ in a specific room or location, ie. bathroom, kitchen
- ❏ other _____

W ill it need some fastening to hang it somewhere:
- ❏ magnet
- ❏ Velcro
- ❏ hook
- ❏ metal rings
- ❏ thumb tacks
- ❏ string or cord

h ow frequently will it be used:
- ❏ one time
- ❏ special events
- ❏ regularly scheduled activities
- ❏ all the time

h ow much time do you have to assemble it:
- ❏ a quick emergency
- ❏ need something today
- ❏ soon
- ❏ need major planning

IMPLEMENTATION

W hen and how will the tool be introduced to students:

W hat student response is expected:

W hat demonstration or prompting is likely to be needed:

W hat student performance will be considered acceptable or successful:

SELECTING SYMBOLS FOR EFFECTIVE COMMUNICATION

Your communication tool samples contain a variety of symbols. Which ones are the best to use?

There are lots of possibilities. It is critical to make selections that are easily understood by the students. Sometimes people create arbitrary rules for themselves about how to do this. Let's get rid of some unnecessary constraints.

Myth #1: All the symbols need to be the same format.

Some people think that if you select black and white line drawings, then everything needs to be in that format. If you select photographs, that is all you should use. This is not true. In fact, providing a variety of symbols makes tools interesting and easier to interpret.

Myth #2: It is necessary to move up to increasingly more abstract representations.

Again, not true. There is nothing to be gained by making tools that challenge the student's comprehension. This is not the forum for teaching that skill.

My students are not consistent in their response to different forms. I'm not sure I know which choice is best.

It is challenging to guess how students will interpret visual forms. Remember that we use language to help us interpret abstract figures. When we look at line drawings we use language to evaluate the shape to decide what concept or action is being represented. Students who have language impairments may not be using the same strategies that we do to analyze what they see. When looking at the same picture, some of our students may just assign meaning to an abstract shape. If that is their style of functioning, you can guess that a collection of pictures with many stick figures will begin to all look alike. Ask yourself what it looks like to the student.

There is a continuum of complexity of visual symbols. Real objects and photographs are generally considered more concrete. Signs, logos, drawings and written words represent higher levels of abstraction. It is risky to assume what forms a student understands easily without exposing him to a variety of visual materials to observe his response to them.

Using a variety of picture styles when creating communication tools can make them more effective. The variety can provide easier scanning and recognition of the symbols. Uniformity is not necessary.

How do you interpret pictures? Do you use language strategies to analyze the configuration and derive meaning from the configuration? How would you interpret the pictures without using language?

When preparing tools for a group of students, develop a format that uses symbols that will be understood by all of them. A combination of pictures and words will be recognized by most.

Is that why you talk about using a variety of visual forms?

Yes. Since we don't know what part of the visual symbols students are responding to, it seems sensible to produce some variety to support easier recognition. Remember the elements of size, shape and color. Use them carefully to produce visual variety. Using a variety of mediums from photos and labels to line drawings and written words, will produce different results from using just one medium.

Aren't some of these visual forms easier to use than others?

It is certainly easier to put information in writing or to photocopy some pictures from a prepared book than it is to go through the process of taking a lot of photos. It is not bad to use the easier forms as long as they meet the student's needs. A well-developed system may use some of each.

REMEMBER: Choosing visual forms that are quickly and easily identified by students will increase the immediate effectiveness of visual tools.

THE POINT IS: The selection of visual forms is an important element in the development of visual tools. Choosing forms that are too difficult for the student to understand will undermine your goals.

Selecting forms that the student easily understands will enhance the communication goals from using visual tools.

You may be surprised at what visual symbols from the environment are either recognized or not recognized by each student.

Make selection of visual symbols a student activity. Photos, drawings and package labels can be supplemented with free literature from businesses, free samples, or plastic bags filled with discovered treasures. All these visual things will stimulate communication, which is the ultimate goal.

Just as a student can demonstrate difficulty with reading comprehension, he can also experience an inability to make meaning from pictures. A student may not magically understand just because you present a drawing instead of a written word. There are numbers of picture or graphic systems commercially available ranging in abstractness from actual photographs to three dimensional drawings to stick figures to abstract symbols representing words and concepts. Although the preprinted symbols are easy to access for a teacher, choosing a system that is too abstract for a targeted student will undermine the main purpose of developing visual systems. The more abstract our visual representations, the more we are assuming about the student's ability to see, interpret, make meaning, and take action.

DO'S AND DON'TS FOR MAKING SUCCESSFUL TOOLS

Once you use the Guide for Planning Communication Tools to target areas for support with visual tools, you can tap your artistic creativity. Do not be intimidated by the word "artistic". Effective visual tools do not need to be elaborate. In fact, simple is usually better. Here are some ideas to ensure your successful effort.

DO: MAKE AIDS FOR A PURPOSE
Educators can spend hours of time making cute things that will not accomplish effective communication enhancement. It is important to define the specific problem, situation, or need to be addressed. Then the aid can be developed to meet that need.

Visual Communication Tools are different from decorative bulletin boards. Classrooms that are well designed to support communication often reduce or totally eliminate decorative boards to leave room for the tools that are used to enhance classroom communication.

DO: THINK THROUGH CAREFULLY HOW YOU WILL USE THE TOOL BEFORE MAKING IT
Who will use it? Where will it be used? When will it be referred to? Where will it be kept or stored? How will it be used? What will the person who is using it say and do? The Guide for Planning Communication Tools will guide you through a series of questions to help make those decisions.

DO: CONSIDER USING COMBINATIONS OF PICTURES AND WRITTEN WORDS

It is easy to assume that because students are readers they should be presented only with grade level written material. Think about how the advertising world relies on pictures and logos and simple written material to establish instant recognition. Visual tools should also be designed so that they can be identified and interpreted easily and with as little effort as possible. Remember, the visual tools are a means to another end. This is not the time for in depth reading instruction. If students get bogged down in trying to read or interpret aids, the other goals that are being addressed will not be achieved as easily. Readers perform with more confidence when using a combination of pictures and written words. Remember, instant recognition is the goal.

Most "nonreaders" really do some reading. From recognizing the logos of their favorite fast food restaurants to selecting their choices of cereals and soft drinks, they do get meaning from some forms of printed or written material. Students who would not be considered candidates for more traditional reading instruction have been observed to develop some functional reading skills by being exposed to written language used as a part of visual tools. Comprehension of the words they learn is excellent because those words have been learned in highly contextual situations.

DO: MAKE VISUAL TOOLS SIMPLE BUT CLEAR

The goal is to create displays that are uncomplicated but still accomplish the objective.

THE PICTURES:

- make sure they are easily identifiable by whoever is using the tool

- use one picture for one concept so the message is communicated efficiently (Most visual tools are developed for the purpose of enhancing communication efficiently rather that teaching more specific language structures.)

⬇ Too Much ⬇

| please | tie | □ | my | running shoes |

⬇ Better ⬇

please tie my shoes

dress, wear

put your shirt on

THE WORDS:

■ if the pictures are already labeled, change the words to match what you say when you use the picture

■ write words that say exactly what the speaker says

■ whole sentences are not necessary

■ sometimes single words are enough

■ be sure to give enough information

■ make sure there is enough writing so that anyone using the aid will understand exactly what the script and purpose is for using that particular item

THE LOOK:

■ consider using *some* color to enhance recognition

■ avoid the temptation to color and "cutsie" the pictures too much

DO: BE CREATIVE AND OBSERVANT WHEN CONSIDERING SIZES OF VISUAL AIDS

Watch how students respond to the tools that are available to them. Your choice of size is determined by:

■ location

■ how tools will be used

■ age of student

■ skill level of student

■ what the student responds to best

■ small tools can be conveniently carried wherever you go

■ tools housed in a 3-ring binder are harder to lose than little cards and pieces of paper

■ large pictures may be easier for some students to recognize than smaller ones

■ tools for the community need to be big enough for easy comprehension by others and yet small enough that they aren't inconvenient and don't cause inappropriate attention

DO: MAKE A "ROUGH DRAFT" AND TRY IT OUT IF YOU ARE UNSURE OF HOW THE DETAILS WILL WORK

One of the greatest disappointments is to spend a lot of time putting together a project that doesn't work. That can deflate anyone's enthusiasm. Sometimes it is hard to predict how students will handle or understand something new presented to them. Will pictures or photos or written words work best? What symbols will the students understand most easily? What size do things need to be? The "rough draft" strategy gives you a chance to try things out a bit and experiment to see what system will work best for your situation. Then things can be done in a more permanent form or laminated or made more beautiful.

DO: TACKLE ONE PROJECT AT A TIME

The fastest way to become discouraged is to photocopy a million pictures and become confused and frustrated by a huge pile of unfinished "stuff" on your desk. Once a person understands the concept of visual communication tools, it is easy to identify a number of projects that would be valuable in a typical classroom. Develop a plan. Then tackle one project at a time.

DO: PRIORITIZE

Identify which aids will be most useful for the most pressing needs and begin there. Frequently people begin by developing a daily schedule system for classroom organization. Many other classroom management tools that are developed are related in some way to that schedule. Another place to begin is developing tools to manage specific behavior problems. Addressing behaviors can be helpful but may also need to be supported by some classroom organization strategies or information giving strategies put into place simultaneously.

> *When developing a tool to use for art activities, the teacher automatically dug out a large piece of poster board and created an aid to hang on the wall. Once it was in place it became obvious that since the work table was in the middle of the room, it was not convenient for the students to refer to the wall chart. Poster board size was too big to place on the table. After rethinking the situation, the teacher redeveloped the tool into small cards that would sit on the table.*

Visual Strategies For Improving Communication

DO: RECOGNIZE ALL VISUAL TOOLS DO NOT NEED TO BE CREATED EQUAL

How much time do you have to create a tool? How frequently will it be used? Some systems call for longer planning and more elaborate preparation. Then there are tools created in one minute to meet an immediate need. They can be simple and yet most helpful in handling some of life's emergencies. A quick instant photo can save the day, even for a student whose general ability level would warrant more sophistication. A non-reader may get along just fine with a stick figure and a couple of words written on a piece of paper in an emergency.

DO: CONSIDER INCLUDING STUDENTS IN THE DEVELOPMENT OF THE AIDS

Depending on the level of understanding of individual students, they can often benefit from being a part of, or witnessing, the development of the communication tools. Rather than presenting a totally completed tool to a student, assemble it in front of him, with his attention or assistance.

- let them watch as you take the photo and mount it on a page
- let them see you cut (or help you cut) the picture off a package to place on a menu board
- when looking through a book for a choice of pictures to use, have them help you select which pictures
- ask them if they want just written words or a combination of words and pictures
- ask them what they think the pictures should say
- ask them what else they want placed on a visual tool-what do they want help remembering
- ask them to help decide where to put tools for easy retrieval

As students participate in the development and planning of visual aids they understand the usefulness and acquire a different sense of ownership for the tools.

DO: BUILD YOUR COMMUNICATION TOOLS PIECE BY PIECE

Don't feel "the whole thing" has to be put together before it can be used. Presenting too much to students at one time can be overwhelming and less effective than presenting a little piece at a time. For example: When making a list of classroom rules you might begin by introducing one. Then in a day or a week, add a second rule to the list, and so forth. When making a choice board for requesting snacks or leisure activities, you can begin with one or two choices. Others can be added one at a time. Have the students watch as you add the pieces to the board. Some people begin creating a daily schedule by scheduling a portion of the day and then gradually adding the extras until the right number of sections have been added to the schedule for comfortable functioning.

Educators tend to have a sense of "compulsive completion" that is not necessary when developing visual aids. The best visual tools are those that are in constant transition. Some tools need to continually increase in size to accommodate for student growth and needs. In other cases, aids such as task organizers can gradually downsize as students develop more independence in accomplishing tasks. Classroom tools need to change as circumstances dictate. The least effective aids are those that are put together so permanently that they are never reevaluated or changed.

DON'T: BECOME DISCOURAGED IF YOU TRY SOMETHING THAT DOES NOT WORK IMMEDIATELY

Many visual tools create instant comprehension and improvement in performance when they are introduced to students. That part is exciting. Then there are students and situations when the instant success is not observed. Don't be tempted to throw out the system too quickly. If that happens:

- evaluate the *form* of the tools used. Does the student easily understand the symbols used?

- don't forget that *teaching* is a necessary part of the process. These students will need more systematic teaching to acquire the skills.

Shawn did not appear to be responding to the visual tools that had been introduced to him in the classroom. His teacher was becoming discouraged until one day Shawn's mother reported this event. Last night as they were driving on an errand, Shawn noticed a "no left turn" sign and announced "no going out the door". His teacher had been using a NO sign posted on the classroom door to communicate to Shawn that he could not run out of the classroom. Shawn's teacher was convinced that this "visual stuff" was beginning to make sense to him.

THE POINT IS:

- there is no single way to develop visual communication tools

- it is necessary to be creative so your efforts will produce tools that will effectively meet your student's individual needs

- visual tools can come in many sizes and shapes

- visual tools do not need to be limited to standard, traditional formats

- these tools take time to make

- the time invested to develop visual supports will be repaid many times in improved communication and behavior

Chapter 9

The Nuts And Bolts

MATERIALS AND SUPPLIES

Creating Visual Communication Tools requires some supplies and materials that may not commonly be found in the teacher's desk. Most are easily obtained from office supply or photo supply stores and are of minimal expense.

CAMERA:

A good camera is the most costly but most necessary part of a teacher's repertoire. Many teachers and therapists view the idea of the school purchasing such an item an impossibility. What a challenge for the art of persuasion! Having an attitude that cameras and film are necessary teaching supplies just like paper or glue can help convince the people in charge of budgets that a camera is not just a toy or a frill. Camera and film purchases may actually replace other materials purchases. They may end up replacing high-tech augmentative devices that are actually much costlier.

NOTE: A camera is a one time expenditure. Film, on the other hand, is an ongoing expense. Some educators have developed creative ways to provide financial support for the necessary finances. Writing grants, soliciting donations from stores or photo supply places, requesting donations from PTA's and other organizations, and creative substitutions with budget directors have all been methods to accomplish this purpose.

CHOICE #1: 35mm camera...for the real "photo buff"

A standard 35mm camera with interchangeable lenses offers the most flexibility and creativity. There are many good brands on the market. Consider a standard 50mm lens for larger shots and a *CLOSE-UP* (macro) lens for taking close up photos of small objects. Some of these cameras come with automatic features so a novice photographer does not have to worry about setting all the buttons and dials that a more experienced photographer loves to play with. These cameras are the most expensive and generally a little larger, but also the most versatile. It may take a bit of practice to feel comfortable with one, but they will also produce the best results.

CHOICE #2: 35mm camera...for the novice photographer

For the average picture taker, there are now a large selection of the smaller 35mm cameras that are totally automatic. They load their own film, make all the technical adjustments, and even brush their own teeth when necessary. They are less expensive and easy to use. The shortcoming is that most of them do not have interchangeable lenses. Consequently, they may not be able to do justice to the close-up photo needs you may have.

Look for a camera that has a built in close-up, macro or telephoto feature for taking your specialized pictures. You need to be able to take close pictures of small objects such as a spoon. Consult a sales person or the camera instructions about the focusing range of the camera. Each camera has a distance range where pictures will be in focus. One may take in-focus pictures when the camera is eighteen inches away from the object. Another camera may produce out-of-focus pictures unless the object you are photographing is at least four feet away from the camera. Keep that focusing distance in mind as you look through the camera at a small object. You will get a sense of how much of the frame will be filled with the object. The most effective photos will be those where the frame is at least half filled with the object.

A camera with the features to take close-up pictures will probably be at the higher end of the price range, but that feature will be well worth it when you begin taking photographs.

NOTE: *The close-up capability of the camera that you choose has been stressed. Think about the types of things you may have cause to photograph. This author spends lots of time taking pictures of spoons and peanut butter jars and other small items. When you shop for a camera, be sure to tell the sales person what you will be doing and that you want to get a camera that has the capacity to take pictures of small things clearly. If you are spending the money, make sure you get something that will produce results that will be acceptable for your needs. Trying to save a few dollars here may make you "penny wise and pound foolish."*

A 35mm camera will produce substantially better pictures than the instamatic and disc type cameras. The pictures will be larger and clearer and you will have better close range potential.

CHOICE #3 Polaroid Camera

The convenience of getting an instant print frequently out weighs any benefits from other cameras. With a Polaroid you can take the pictures and use them right now. That value is extremely important when using the picture to enhance immediate communication.

Polaroid also makes some camera versions that have a close-up capability. Check it out carefully. Unfortunately, the ones that take better close-ups are on the higher end of the cost spectrum, but the ease of taking the pictures you need and putting them to work immediately is invaluable.

THE *NEW* FAVORITE CHOICE

The current favorite camera is rapidly becoming a **digital camera.** They are extremely easy to use and cost efficient in the long term. You need to have:

1. A computer that has the capacity to support a camera (both Macintosh and IBM formats can do this)

2. A printer: a good color ink jet printer works great for photos

3. A drawing program is not necessary but very helpful to support your creative talents

How they work: You take pictures just like you would with a regular camera. The digital camera has no film in it. The pictures are recorded inside the camera. Then you take your camera back to the computer. For some cameras, you hook a cable from the camera to the computer, do a few simple button pushing things and the pictures transfer from the camera to the computer. Some of the newer cameras skip the cable step. Instead, they have a computer disk inside the camera that you take out and slide into the computer just like other disks to load information. Once the disk is in the computer, your pictures get loaded onto the hard drive just like other information.

Once digital photos are on the computer hard drive, you can perform many functions with them. They can be reduced, enlarged and manipulated just like other art work. You can transport them into a drawing program to be placed along side other art work and print for creating visual tools. They can be stored on your hard drive so you can go back to use them over again.

Just like other cameras, digital cameras are produced with different levels of complexity. It will be good to shop a bit and have a salesperson explain the details of the choices you have. When looking at these cameras, be sure to find out about wide angle and close-up capability. Make sure the camera can take the kinds of pictures you need. Tell the salesperson that you want to take pictures of small items (like a spoon or a piece of candy) or crop a part out of a bigger picture and blow them up to an 8" x 10" size. Although most or all of these cameras will be able to do that, the cameras with greater zoom possibilities will do a better job. Otherwise, you may end up producing very fuzzy bigger pictures. Just like buying cars and clothes and other things, the greatest bargain is no bargain if it doesn't meet your needs.

Although the initial cost of a digital camera is considerably more than other cameras, there can be a long term cost savings because there are no film or developing expenses over time. Consider putting one on your "wish list" and see what happens. Beware: There is such rapid development in this kind of computer equipment that old technology is really old. If you are tempted to skimp, your equipment can be outdated before you begin.

SOURCES FOR PICTURES:

Speech - Language Pathologist:

This is the best place to begin. They tend to have reams of files and programs and books with resources to begin your search. The problem you will encounter is that many of the resources they have will not fit your specific needs for developing visual tools. Many of the picture programs they have may have been designed for teaching specific articulation or language skills and will not offer the subject matter you need.

A number of companies have books and card sets with pictures appropriate for creating visual communication tools. Most Speech-Language Pathologists have cabinets full of them. With the help of a good photocopy machine many sources can be tapped for your creative expression. The artwork that appears to be most effective is simple drawings that are very realistic looking.

Several companies have recently developed picture dictionaries and training pictures on computer disc. The computer offers numerous possibilities for rapid assembly of communication tools.

Other Sources:

Photocopy photographs for an interesting way to duplicate them. If they are not too dark they can produce a very acceptable picture. You may need to put the photocopy machine on a "light" setting.

- magazine and newspaper ads
- store coupons
- package wrappers
- pictures from the containers items come in

Advertising pictures are helpful resources for your visual collection because they are colorful and lifelike. They provide instant recognition for most students. If you have access to a photocopy machine that reduces and enlarges or one that reproduces in color you have some extra potential with these.

Draw:

Don't flinch if you don't consider yourself an artist. Even people who are non-artists can usually draw well enough to create simple pictures for visual communication tools. Uncomplicated shapes can communicate the essentials for most needs. Don't discount this idea until you try it.

OTHER MATERIALS TO HELP MAKE VISUAL TOOLS:

plastic page protectors

Office supply and photo stores carry plastic page protectors for slides, photos, and papers. They come in heavy weight and lighter weight plastic and usually have holes punched along the side so they will fit in a 3-ring binder. Consider the weight of the plastic in relationship to the students you will use them with. Some students definitely need the heavy weight plastic!

Plastic pages come with varying numbers of slots on each page. Slide protectors have 20 slots on a page (perfect for holding two inch pictures). Photo protectors have 4 to 6 slots on a page, and whole page protectors can be used to slide in a whole 8 1/2 x 11 piece of paper (more convenient than laminating because you can pull the page out to make additions or changes easily). Each size and style provides for different needs depending on the style of aid you are creating.

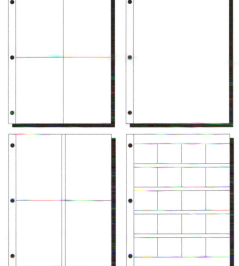

laminating

Protecting visual tools helps preserve them. Soft lamination provides good protection. Hard lamination makes tools very sturdy-particularly good for students who require more durability.

photo books

Small, one picture to a page, pocket photo books (like a Grandma's Brag Book) that contain about 10-20 pages are convenient for putting together many personal aids, cookbooks, and task analyzers.

ring-binders

These come in a variety of sizes. Classic 8 1/2 x 11 inch three-ring binders are handy for carrying many communication tools. The size is a bit bigger than some people would like, but people find that the inconvenience of size is quickly replaced by the convenience of always being able to find the book...the bigger it is, the harder to lose. (some people even need neon binders!)

subject dividers

Used in the ring-binders, they are helpful for categorizing pages used for different purposes or locations. They are effective for organizing a three-ring binder for more efficient use. It makes finding a needed page a bit easier.

self stick notes

Handy to cover pictures or items that are not there.

metal rings
Used to hold groups of pictures or cards together.

hooks
Magnets or self stick types are handy to attach to walls, cabinets doors, etc. Helps to keep tools in the locations where you will use them. (Found in bathroom, kitchen or office departments in the store.)

Velcro
A most marvelous invention! Helpful to stick tools wherever you want them. Velcro makes it easy to remove a tool to carry to a new location, or put closer to a person to make communication more effective.

magnets or magnetic tape
When placed on the back of visual tools, the tape creates tools that can be easily attached to metal, i.e., your filing cabinets or storage cabinets.

apron with big pockets
A great tool for teachers who like to carry their most frequently used tools within reach at all times.

storage box with small drawers
Found in hardware departments. Perfect for storing pictures, particularly those used for the scheduling systems recommended in this book.

file boxes and storage containers of various sizes
Convenient storage of visual tools is essential for their effective use. Many choices for storage containers work, depending on size, shape, and location of the tools.

mini flashlight
Used as an attention getting device. Shine it on the place you want student to attend to help him focus on specific visual cues used in a communication exchange.

PHOTOGRAPHY 101

Photographs are the easiest and clearest symbols to use for many visual communication needs. Unfortunately, many people experience less than successful results from the use of photos because the quality of the pictures does not meet the needs of the students for efficient understanding. Taking pictures for visual communication tools is somewhat different from taking casual snapshots. A few guidelines for the non-photographer will help produce quality photos to ensure a highly effective communication system.

IDENTIFY THE CRITICAL ELEMENT:
What are you taking a picture of? Ask yourself what part is the critical element that the student will focus on to understand and interpret most easily?

Taking pictures of objects is fairly easy. A close photo of just the object is most effective. Try to isolate the object you are photographing so it will be the main or only thing in the picture.

Photographing actions and places is more difficult. For example: if you wanted a photo to indicate the student was going to gym, would you take a picture of the big empty room, or the door to the gym, or some of the equipment in the gym, or the gym teacher holding a piece of gym equipment the student was familiar with?

If you wanted a picture to indicate the student was going to butter toast would you photograph the whole kitchen including the counter with the toaster, plate, knife, butter, and student all in one picture? Would you zoom in to show a pair of hands holding a knife while putting butter on the toast?

If you were taking a photograph to indicate a trip to a favorite fast food restaurant would you highlight the front of the building with the person standing there, the sign in front of the place or the cashier taking an order? (Or would you forget the photo and use a copy of the logo of the restaurant that the students recognize?)

Instead of photographing the environment, would a picture of the favorite purchase be more meaningful? Which would the child recognize better; a picture of the sign at the ice cream store or a picture of an ice cream cone? (If you use the picture of ice cream, will that confuse him if you go to that place to have a sandwich instead of ice cream? Or will he be confused if you go to a different store for the ice cream?)

NOTE: There is a line of thinking that suggests it is desirable to photograph the student *doing* the activity. For some students and situations this may accomplish a helpful image, for example, a picture of the student performing an action like sitting or lying down. Using this approach of photographing the student using the objects can create a problem. It results in the *critical element* being very small. When students are looking at these photos they can have a difficult time focusing on the critical element because it is such a small part of the photo. In addition, experience has revealed that *most students respond better to the pictures that replicate what the student sees.* He doesn't see himself doing the actions....but he does see the objects involved with the activity. When photographing actions with objects, the most effective photos are those that highlight the object so it can be quickly and easily identified.

When deciding what to photograph, pick something:

- that is as universal as possible
- that won't require frequent replacement
- that will communicate the intent as clearly as possible

Try to isolate the critical element and highlight it in the photo. If too many things are in a picture the student may focus on a different part than we want him to.

play the keyboard

horses

Or

keyboard

Or

horses

SHOOT CLOSE UP:

One of the biggest mistakes non-photographers make is taking a picture too far away. Try to fill up at least two-thirds of the picture frame with the essential part of the picture. Otherwise, that critical element gets lost and is more difficult for everyone to identify. If you don't shoot close up, the critical element may be only a fraction of an inch in size in the picture. When taking portraits of people, a waist up shot is generally preferable to a full body shot. When shooting actions, zero in on the critical part of the movement or the object involved.

Be aware of what distance you must be from the subject to have your picture in focus. With some cameras you can be in focus when you are just inches away from your subject. Other cameras will not be in focus if you are closer that three or four feet. Make sure to know the limits of your camera so lots of film isn't wasted.

ELIMINATE THE BACKGROUND:

Look at what is behind your subject. If you are taking pictures of people, try to position them so you have plain walls or uncluttered space behind them. When taking pictures of objects, try to eliminate surrounding distractions. To make a picture of an object stand out visually, try putting the object on a piece of poster board to provide a clear background with a contrasting color. Remember that what you see in the viewfinder of the camera will help you know what will be in the photo.

too far away

too much background

better

WATCH YOUR LIGHTING:

Unless you are using a fancy camera, most indoor pictures will need a flash. Many of the newer cameras have built-in automatic flashes. Look for one of these if you are a "flash forgetter".

Don't position your subject so you aim your camera directly at a window. The light coming in from the window will throw off the camera's light metering systems. You will end up with lots of light from the window and the subject will be too dark and hard to see. To adjust for that, just turn or move yourself slightly so your camera is not aiming directly at the window.

When shooting outdoors, avoid shooting directly into the sun or having the sun shine directly on peoples faces (or you will record beautiful squints). Contrary to popular belief, you don't have to be standing in the sun. Modest shade can produce nice pictures.

MAKE SURE YOU HAVE FILM IN THE CAMERA:

(Guess why this one was included!) Surprisingly, this is a frequent problem. Many cameras have a little window that tells you if there is film in the camera. Find it. Most cameras have a counter to record how many pictures have been taken or how many are left on a roll of film. Unfortunately, many of those counters will work even if there is no film in the camera. It is particularly difficult when more than one person shares the use of a camera. Communicate!

HOLD THE CAMERA STILL AND SHOOT:

It is amazing how many photos are ruined because the photographer jiggled. Sometimes people lift the camera and shoot quickly before they are done moving. *Hint:* Hold your elbows close to your body to help you steady the camera.

TAKE GENERIC PHOTOS WHEN POSSIBLE:

It is wonderful to personalize the communication system for each student, however, *over-personalization* can create much unnecessary work for the teacher. For example, if you are photographing a series of jobs for a MINI-SCHEDULE for lunch preparation, is it necessary to take a picture of Jenny setting the table, then John setting the table, then Ralph setting it and so forth for each member of your class? If you take a generic picture of someone's hands setting the table will your students understand? Generic or non personal photos can be duplicated for all the students in your class. This can be a huge time and cost savings compared to having to take a complete set of pictures for each student *if it is appropriate for them*. There are some students who need things very personalized. For others it makes no difference.

ORGANIZE YOUR NEGATIVES:

Figure out a convenient way to store your negatives. It is not unusual to want duplicate copies of pictures you have already taken, and frustration develops when the negatives can't be found. Making duplicates is cheaper than retaking pictures, so organization has both financial and time saving rewards.

PRACTICAL TIPS FOR DEVELOPING VISUAL TOOLS

People who have been making visual tools for use in their classrooms have passed on lots of little ideas that have made their own results more effective. Consider these.

PICTURES:

Don't forget color as a tool to enhance visual tools.

- Try coloring the background of black & white drawings instead of coloring the foreground. Background color enhances visibility. The color yellow produces the best visibility.

- Don't color all the pictures on a page.

- Cut photographs to eliminate extraneous background.

- For rapid recognition or categorization, try color coding pictures.

Don't hesitate to produce multi-media systems. Written words, photographs, newspaper pictures, labels from packages and line drawings can all be part of the same tool to communicate.

Pages packed full of abstract black and white line drawings can be difficult to scan. Use color or varied symbols to create visual interest and assist scanning.

Use lines or grids to organize a page. It is easier to scan a page that has lines to assist the eye.

COMMUNICATION BOOKS:
Color code pages in bigger communication books for easier retrieval of the page you are looking for. (i.e. schedule pages are blue, leisure pages are pink, workshop pages are green, etc.).

Consider dividers to separate the sections in a bigger book that holds a number of pages.

MEASURING:
Two inch pictures may not fit into two inch drawers or two inch picture holders unless they are trimmed first.

VISUAL TOOL BACKING:
When making pieces for students to manipulate and slide into holders or slots, experiment by backing the pieces with index cards, tag board, or poster board weights.

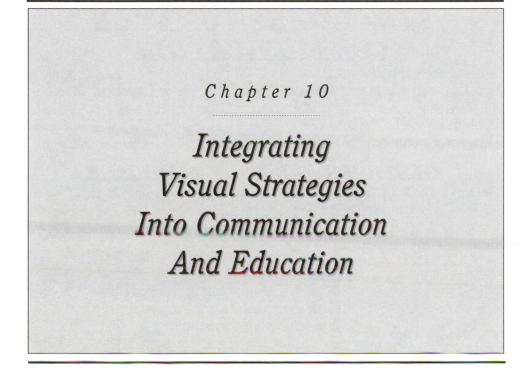

Chapter 10

Integrating Visual Strategies Into Communication And Education

Communication is the foundation for education. The development of effective communication skills determines social interaction, precedes acquisition of academic skills, and affects student's self-management and behavior. Communication competence cannot be assumed. The student's participation and progress in the educational environment needs to be evaluated within a communication framework. When communication needs are identified, new skills can be taught. The most effective classrooms are those that provide the ongoing support necessary to enhance communication skills. Using visual strategies to support communication is a technique that has provided an abundance of results for the effort.

STRATEGIES TO TEACH COMMUNICATION

A discussion of using visual communication tools risks focusing on the development of augmentative aids at the expense of forgetting to emphasize the use of the most convenient and effective tool available: the human body. The interpretation and use of nonverbal cues to support communication is essential to developing effective exchanges.

GESTURES AND BODY LANGUAGE

Gestures and body language are tools that are key elements for establishing attention and clarifying communication. The range of non verbal skills that will enhance communication interactions include interpretation and use of:

Gestures that do not mean anything do not help communication. One teacher was observed waving his arms all over when giving directions to his students. The problem was that the arm movements were just random. They did not communicate any special meaning. As a result they ended up being confusing and distracted the students from the real communication intended.

A cow and flies using nonverbal communication.
By Joseph Anderson, age 13
© 1990 Imaginart

- body orientation
- establish or change proximity
- eye contact, eye gaze, gaze shift
  - person to person
  - identifying a referent
  - focusing on mutual referent
- facial expressions
- hand/body movements
  - pointing
  - reaching,touching
  - pushing,pulling
  - gestural reference to something in the environment

When communicating *to* students, an animated approach is frequently a help. That does not mean using random movements to the point of distraction or confusion. It does not mean to become excessively verbal. It does mean using your body to get the student's attention and using exaggerated gestures to communicate your meaning. Effective gestures include:

- a very obvious head shake to communicate "NO"
- standing right in front of a student to get his attention
- holding an object right in the student's line of sight
- putting something down in an exaggerated fashion to demonstrate where to put it
- holding up your hands to ask "where"
- exaggerating a shoulder movement and shaking your head to communicate "I don't know"

- pointing to the item you want the student to attend to
- pushing an object away
- tapping someone on the shoulder to get their attention
- taking a person by the hand to lead them to a location
- using a hand gesture to tell someone to come here

These are common gestures that communicate their messages quite effectively.

But isn't it better to work on more sophisticated communication strategies?

No. Many students who experience autism and others who demonstrate moderate to severe communication difficulties do not understand or use gestures adequately. The group of students who display a weakness in this area can benefit greatly from specific training to teach the skills they haven't picked up incidentally. Teach them how to interpret your body language. Then show them how to use natural gestures to enhance their own communication attempts.

> *Even students who talk may need gesture training.*

Difficulties with non verbal communication significantly affects a student's communication effectiveness. Responding to and using a gestural system places communication on a more concrete level.

Intervention plans that attempt to teach symbolic skills at a higher level than the student can comfortably understand may decrease, rather than increase spontaneous participation. Teaching effective non verbal skills can increase spontaneity.

Well, my students already talk a lot. Isn't working on gestures taking a step backward?

Remember, we are still talking about both receptive and expressive communication skills. Focusing training to teach students to understand your non verbal communication will have a major relationship to increasing comprehension and overall communication effectiveness. Improving a student's ability to use non verbal communication isn't stepping backwards. It is helping him become more capable.

Do you have any suggestions about how to teach those non verbal communication skills?

Keep in mind that some of the best teaching strategies are non verbal, or accomplished with limited verbal input. Here are a few ideas to help.

When communicating *to* the student:

1. Model the gestures. When you are communicating to him, get close to the student. Very close. Get yourself into his visual field. Make your own gestures very clear and distinct.

2. Exaggerate the gestures and the language to accompany them. Make them take a long time. (Remember the students who have difficulty establishing attention.) For example: If you are telling the student "NO," bend down to his level, shake your head several times while you say , "NOOOOOO." Verbalize just the words that are critical to the communication. Make it simple.

When helping the student communicate:

1. Use non verbal prompting. When it is appropriate for a student to use a gesture, visually or physically prompt him. Don't *tell* him what to do. Don't say, "Johnny, shake your head." Instead, try to model the gesture and words he needs to use for him to imitate. Do it with him. Do it long enough so he can imitate and join in to do it simultaneously with you. If that doesn't produce the desired result, try physically prompting him. Touch his head enough to help him shake his head while you say the word that he is communicating. Any words that are said should be the words he would be using to communicate his intent.

Waiting is an important element in communication. After communicating a message, it is critical to give the student enough time to receive the information, process, and then formulate a response. If students don't respond immediately, most people are tempted to jump in and repeat the message too quickly. For some students, a responding time of five or ten seconds or more may be necessary for real participation. For the teacher, waiting five or ten seconds may seem unbearable.

2. Watch for "two-people" situations to teach gestures. It is frequently difficult to prompt a student if you are the person he is attempting to communicate with. Try to take advantage of situations where the student is communicating with one person and another person can do the prompting. For example: If the student needs to tell the teacher to "come here," the aide (standing behind the student) would take the student's hand and physically prompt the student to take the teacher's hand to pull the teacher to the destination. The prompter does not participate as part of the interaction. The prompter's only job is to non verbally guide the student to perform the action. Another example: If the student wants the toy that another student has, stand behind him and physically prompt him to put his hands out or point to make the request. One more example: When the student is standing near the adult but doesn't know how to get the adult's attention, model or physically prompt the student to touch the person's arm or tap the person's shoulder to get their attention.

UTILIZING THE NATURAL ENVIRONMENT

A discussion about specially prepared visual tools risks overlooking the natural environment. Don't forget to make use of what is already available around you. Signs, posters, objects, and anything else you can see, point to, touch or hold all make visual tools to clarify your communication. Teach your students to utilize these tools.

Some students need to learn to focus attention on a mutual referent. Remember that visual tools that are physically close to the student may be easier to see and interpret than things far away. You may have to get very close to make sure the student is paying attention to the communication supports.

THE POINT IS:
The most basic Visual Communication Tools are the body of the communicator and those things that are present in his immediate environment. Before developing ways to augment communication with other supports, it is efficient and prudent to make best use of what naturally already exists. The improvement of a natural gesture system will undergird and support all other communication training.

DEVELOPING A COMMUNICATION BASED CLASSROOM: CRITICAL ELEMENTS FOR SUCCESS

Developing an educational program for students who experience moderate to severe communication disorders requires an environment that will effectively support the development of communication skills. A "communication based" classroom is one in which the fostering of communication skills is of primary focus. It recognizes that efficient development of other functional or academic skills is dependent on the student's communication ability. Communication is a foundation for everything else that is to be accomplished. Here is how it's done.

CRITICAL ELEMENTS IN A COMMUNICATION BASED CLASSROOM

1. Place the educational focus on communication development FIRST. Design the flow of the classroom, the schedule, timing and other activities so the teaching of communication skills can assume primary importance.

2. Design the level of communication in the classroom to match the student's functioning level. The goal is to begin at the level the student can perform and then move him up the "rungs of the ladder" one at a time. If the communication in the environment is too sophisticated for the student, he is outdone before he begins. His performance will be fragmented.

3. Allow time for communication. Design both structured and unstructured activities to allow for communication training. Make sure there are enough unstructured activities planned so the students will have many opportunities for spontaneous communication.

4. Capture the moment. Spontaneity is an essential element. Take advantage of each communication opportunity as it arises. Use those spontaneous situations to teach the skills the student needs to learn.

5. Teach communication skills in natural settings. These students do not generalize well from one situation to another. Attempting to teach communication skills in out-of-context settings will not yield results as effectively as teaching in real, meaningful situations.

6. Integrate communication training into the context of ongoing activities. Communication training should not be saved for 9:45 on Thursday mornings. It needs to be an integral part of everything else that is going on.

7. Develop visual tools as a rich part of the environment to support communication. They are used to schedule events, build routines and support transitions. They give information, communicate rules, and support both receptive and expressive communication.

8. View behavior challenges in the context of communication. Incidents need to be evaluated for the possibility of breakdowns in either understanding or in effectiveness in communicating to others.

9. Specifically teach pragmatic skills. Critical skills include appropriate strategies to get someone's attention, initiating and maintaining a communication exchange, and handling communication breakdowns. The teaching of these skills can be supported visually.

10. Include language activities that place a heavy emphasis on rhythm and rhyme. Music and reading activities that present exaggerated rhythm and rhyme and encourage total body movement are excellent.

11. Ensure a strong relationship between the academic skills taught and the child's experience. Early academics need to have a very functional connection. Develop them to support the student's active participation in real, meaningful experiences.

12. Make sure communication is integrated...not separate. View it as an integral part of almost every activity that the student engages in.

> *It is not possible to present visual symbols for everything that is communicated. Try to use them for those situations that are most likely to need the support: frequent routines, transitions, situations that are likely to create difficulties.*

DO'S AND DON'TS FOR EFFECTIVE IMPLEMENTATION

In the ideal educational environment, the curriculum will focus on the teaching of communication skills as the foundation for other learning. Visual tools and the use of visually mediated communication enhance the learning environment to maximize the student's communication potential. *Using visual tools is not a goal; it is a teaching strategy.* Visual tools support the accomplishment of targeted communication or educational goals. The following tips will help maximize the benefit from using visual strategies.

THINK AHEAD: Spending a bit of time anticipating what the student may need to understand-particularly when anticipating a new situation-can dramatically affect if or how the situation succeeds.

DO: Remember that students need to be taught to use the tools.

Some of them will get the idea right away, as soon as they are shown what to do. Others will need extensive training. In those situations where a tool is put into practice and not found to work, observations frequently reveal that the student wasn't really taught to use it; people just expected him to know what to do. The teaching should replicate the systematic steps necessary to teach other skills to that student.

DO: Introduce the tools to students with a systematic approach.

When introducing a visual tool to younger or lower skilled students the approach is simple.

- Show the tool.
- Gesture or point to show the student where to focus his attention.
- Make sure the student sees the tool.
- Say the script for that communication.
- Immediately prompt or guide the student to perform whatever response is desired from the communication.

Combining a verbal direction with visual support can be the most effective choice, however, bombarding the students by continually repeating the verbal prompts or bombarding with visual stimuli may actually increase the reaction time of the students.

Students who are older or higher skilled may benefit from some conversation about the aid before it is used. Giving them information regarding its purpose and use can create a context of comprehension.

Do's and Don'ts For Effective Implementation

DO: Get the student's attention before using the tool.
It is not uncommon to talk to students from across the room, or when their backs are turned, or when they are looking at something else. In those situations it is difficult to assess how much attention is really focused on you. It is not uncommon, particularly with students who experience autism or have attention disorders, to discover some who do not look as if they are paying attention who really know a lot about what is going on. For most students, however, communication is generally enhanced by the following:

> *Students with gaze avoidance tendencies may be more likely to look at visual symbols than establish visual contact with a person.*

- establishing eye contact or body orientation

- pointing or gesturing to the visual cues you want the student to focus on

- pairing the physical movement with your verbal communication

- encouraging students to point to the visual symbol being used for communication

- encouraging verbal students to repeat the verbal script to assure their attention.

DO: Make sure the student can see the tool when you are using it.
One of the reasons that the visual communication tools are successful is that they provide a stable, *non-transient* message for students. It is necessary to use the aids in a way that enables that visual message to remain visible long enough for the student to see it and process it thoroughly. Leave the aid out in a convenient location so the student can refer to it. Students may refer to the tools frequently to help them keep on task, remember what the communication was or reestablish their attention. To accomplish this:

- Place smaller aides in a location that can be mutually viewed.

- Move physically closer to larger classroom sized aids or those that are displayed in other locations.

- Avoid the temptation to quickly "whip out" the tool and then remove it immediately.

Do's and Don'ts For Effective Implementation

Although it is generally recommended to pair a verbal script with a visual tool, there are occasions when a student appears to perform better with just the visual cue and no verbalization. This may be more likely to happen when a student is experiencing a behavior problem. Careful observation will give you the information you need.

When we feel a need to repeat a direction to a student, it is natural to change the wording, increase the complexity of the language used, or increase the volume. Visual tools help us maintain a concise, systematic presentation.

***Waiting expectantly** is an important part of the communication exchange. When students don't respond or take their turn immediately, it is natural to repeat again and again until they finally respond. These repetitions can actually result in the student taking longer to respond. When using visual tools to communicate messages, it is possible to leave the communication message present long enough for the student to process the information without bombarding him with too much input.*

DO: Use a pointing gesture to clarify your communication.

- Point with your finger in a slow and deliberate manner. Don't remove your hand until you are sure the student has had plenty of time to focus on the communication.
- A "still" point is usually more effective than a "tapping" point.
- Be aware that a tapping point can be done in such an exaggerated way that it actually makes it harder for the student to focus his attention.

DO: Be consistent in the verbal script you speak when using the tool.

When planning your visual supports, plan the language or "scripts" to be used with the aid. The sophistication of the script will parallel the ability level of the students who will use it. The script will be the things that the people will say or communicate while referring to the items on the tool. Using the same script over again helps students learn the routines more rapidly.

Scripts to support the visual aids should be simple and to the point. One or two words or simple phrases are frequently sufficient. Students who experience severe communication difficulties generally function better with simple language.

DO: Limit your verbalization to the script that goes with the tool.

One of the tendencies is to use increasingly more language in an attempt to get students to perform in the required manner. The more difficulty the student has, or the worse his behavior becomes, the more language the teacher may use in an attempt to instill compliance. Avoid using a lot of language. Experience with these students reveals there is generally better student response if the teacher limits his communication to the simple script. If the situation requires more direction, repeat the same simple script again. That emphasizes the communication that needs to be focused on.

DO: Use non verbal prompting to assist students to perform the action communicated by the visual cues.

The goal is for the student to act upon the visual cues and the selected verbal script. Gesturally or physically prompt him if he needs help to do that. Using more language to prompt his performance complicates the communication.

DO: Encourage verbal students to use the script as a form of "self-talk" when using the tools.

The verbalization helps maintain attention, facilitate comprehension, and clarify any misunderstanding in the communication. It is also a step toward independence. Many students use that self-talk as a form of self-regulation.

DO: Teach students to use a pointing gesture that communicates clearly.

An effective point is an asset to students using visual communication tools. A good pointing gesture will enhance and clarify their communication attempts. All pointing gestures do not provide the same support. Many students have a tendency to indicate with several fingers or a whole hand. Using one finger is a more discrete and effective tool. Aim for a pointing movement without a lot of extra motion. There is a temptation for students to perseverate on tapping with their fingers or use a waving gesture and then quickly retract it before people focus on what was referred to. Encourage the pointer to hold the point steady while the communication is going on. That makes it easier for the communication partner to focus on the items targeted. Students need to learn to pay attention to determine if a listener is looking.

DO: Use the tool consistently when you are attempting to establish its use.

The more frequently and consistently it is used, the faster the learning will take place.

DO: Teach the student to maneuver and care for the tools as much as possible.

Make it part of the routine to retrieve the aid, put it in place, turn the pages, and put it away. Making the student responsible for the tools helps foster independence. That is the goal.

> *Teachers who are coping with students who are not doing what they are told to do tend to increase their verbal output. It is a natural response.*

> *Be aware of how you point. Some people point so quickly that their hand is removed before the student can actually benefit from the movement. Another pointing behavior is the "pounding hammer." The person pounds that pointing finger up and down on its target so many times that it actually becomes a distraction. The most effective point is one that is targeted to a specific location and has no movement or just enough movement to get the student's attention.*

> *If the pointing gesture a student uses is not discrete and does not communicate clearly, try to refine it to make it more effective.*

Do's and Don'ts For Effective Implementation

> *Visual communication tools should be in a format to support spontaneous interaction, not get in the way.*

> *There are no prerequisites for using visual communication tools . Many developmental curriculums would have a student work up through a series of matching, object identification and labeling tasks before using pictures for communication purposes. It is suggested that those steps be skipped entirely. Introduce and use visual tools in their communication context immediately.*

> *One group of students who sometimes experience difficulty learning to effectively respond to the use of visual tools are those who were taught to label pictures as a primary language activity. Frequently these students think the **function** of pictures is to label them. They do not understand that the pictures can be used for other functions. It is recommended that you do not focus on teaching labeling to these students. Rather, it is recommended that the names of objects be taught in the context of another function such as making a request or giving information.*

DO: Make sure the tools are simple enough for easy recognition.
Assess the student's response to various types of visual representation. Black and white drawings may be too abstract for some; written language will be satisfactory for others. Some students need real objects while others understand photographs with ease. When in doubt, opt for the simpler choice. Enabling the student to understand and use the system quickly and efficiently is the primary goal.

DO: Remember there are no prerequisites for using visual tools.
The key is to use visual tools that are at a level of comprehension for the student. Strive for the concrete symbols that are most quickly and easily understood. Systematically build in comprehension from the beginning. Create a very clear relationship between the visual cue and the choice or action it represents.

DO: Remember that labeling tasks are not a prerequisite for using visual tools effectively.
In fact, it is recommended that you do not teach labeling as an isolated task. It will serve no function. The students need to learn the communicative function of the visual tools. Teaching them to label pictures or objects will reinforce non communicative language. These students need to be taught to use the labels for a communicative purpose. In that same line of thinking, making lotto games from the pictures you use for communication purposes may confuse students. Remember they need to learn the communication *functions* for those visuals.

DO: Give students time to learn what the tools mean and how to use them.
The most rapid acquisition will come from developing a setting of "errorless learning". The more accurately the student follows the intent of the communication tool, the less time it should take for him to develop the ability to respond appropriately to the communication. For example: When using a schedule or task organizer, once the item is identified, the teacher should give the student as much guidance as is necessary for him to follow that step completely and without error. As the student becomes familiar with the routine the teacher can gradually withdraw the support.

When visual tools are introduced, many students demonstrate rapid comprehension. This results in a short period of prompting before they acquire a basic understanding of the tools. There are other students whose learning curve is much slower. Those slower students eventually acquire ability with the visual tools, but their learning speed with these tools may parallel their learning speed for acquiring other skills. Don't become discouraged when the slower students don't master the skills as quickly as the faster ones. Those slower students will benefit most from the "errorless learning" technique.

DO: Modify the tools as it becomes obvious that changes are necessary.

Once you begin to use an aid, the need for changes sometimes occurs. The most common kinds of changes are related to:

- changes in the tool to better help the student achieve the desired performance

- changes in the student's need because he is learning the skills

The best tools are subject to ongoing modifications. There are situations where visual communication tools have ceased being used because "they didn't work" or "they stopped working". Failure to modify the tool to meet the need is almost always the problem. Changes and alterations in visual communication tools is a common and necessary part of the process.

Any techniques that are introduced into a student's program should be evaluated to determine their effectiveness. When developing the use of visual strategies to support communication, one criteria that helps determine their fit for a particular student is to observe how the student responds to their use. Is there a change in his performance? Does using these tools create a change in the way you interact with each other? Does he gravitate toward those tools? Do you observe him initiating their use? These kinds of questions will be an important part of the assessment process.

JUST A FEW MORE QUESTIONS

I understand the value of using Visually Mediated Communication. What is the long term goal? What outcome should I be aiming for?

The long term goal for students who experience moderate to severe communication disorders is to help them develop an effective, efficient communication system that will enable them to successfully participate in their life activities. Visual tools are supports designed to help students accomplish their goals.

Remember, there is no need to try to eliminate all the visual supports for our students. We all use lots of visual supports to help us handle life's demands efficiently. The long term goal is to teach the student how to access and use visual supports to accomplish their purposes. Students need to learn to recognize their own need and then support themselves by accessing the variety of strategies available to them.

My students are in regular classrooms with other students who don't need all the extra support. Don't they need to learn to function without the supports like the other kids?

Many students in academic curriculums would benefit from learning to use visual strategies to help them study, manage their time, and organize their lives. It doesn't matter if the rest of the class is not using these strategies. Whether or not other students receive the benefit from visual supports, the targeted student needs to learn to independently access the strategies he needs personally to be successful.

---

*Occasionally teachers report having new difficulties with students. These were teachers who had employed numerous visual strategies in their school programs. The students in their rooms had responded well to the use of various visual tools in the past. When analyzing the present behavior problems it became obvious that the teacher originally used the visual tools successfully to handle needs, but then, somewhere along the line, when the behavior problems weren't so bad, they "kinda stopped using them". Not surprisingly, the student's behavior "kinda got worse". After the student displayed improvement in the areas targeted originally for the visual strategies, the need for those strategies **appeared** to diminish. When the aids were eliminated, however, the behaviors increased. As the visual tools were reestablished into the program, there was a corresponding decrease in the targeted behaviors.*

What about my lower skilled students? Won't it make them look more handicapped to keep using visual supports?

Actually, they may look more handicapped without using the supports. One of the goals and purposes in using visual tools is to enable students to function as independently as possible. That means helping them to learn to handle routines and transactions without adult support or intervention. The less they need another person to help them, the more skilled they appear.

Remember, the appearance of visual tools will significantly affect how others perceive them. Make sure they are designed in an unobtrusive, age appropriate style.

I am not a really organized person. How can I make it convenient to use these tools?

Location is the key. Visual tools need to be accessible where you need them. Some rules are appropriately placed on a wall chart and posted in the location where they will be used. Places such as a bulletin board, door, wall or the student's desk may fulfill the need. Other times the visual supports need to be mobile...to be carried throughout the various locations where they need to be used. In some instances it might be appropriate to place the student in charge of his own visual supports. In other situations it may be appropriate to make them the property of the teacher.

It is not necessary to put all the rules and communications for one's life on one page or in one location. Whatever is convenient will have the most chance for success.

> ADVICE: KEEP A COPY OF EVERYTHING YOU DEVELOP. That will make life easier when something gets lost.

Speaking of success...do these visual tools always work? I don't want to do the work if there isn't much chance for success.

Visual tools are not being presented as a "magic cure" for everyone. Their success is dependent upon how they are developed and how they are used. Here are some circumstances where lack of success may occur.

1. The tool doesn't contain the correct information to achieve the desired result. In the planning process, sometimes people misread the situation. Perhaps they have included too much or not enough information. Once the tool is put into use, the students perform differently from what was expected. In these cases it may be necessary to modify or redesign the tool.

2. The student does not understand the symbols that are used. For some reason, the tool does not make sense to the student. (Remember, the purpose of the tools is to help the student understand communication more clearly.) Perhaps the symbols are too abstract or too complicated. Maybe the student does not understand the relationship between the symbols and the actions or choice they represent. Whatever the reason, the tool does not increase understanding.

3. There are too many symbols on a page. If tools are too complicated, students will find them difficult to interpret. Space things out. Too much, too close, or too small takes excessive effort to decipher. Put symbols for different purposes on separate pages or charts for different needs. That helps students organize their thinking.

4. Too many symbols or tools are introduced too quickly. Be careful! Once people understand this concept and see its application, the temptation is to try to do too much too quickly. Even when there are several communication needs, the tools need to be introduced one at a time. Take the time to teach the students how to use each one. Develop some connection with one before you add more. One teacher introduced a book with thirty pages of rules to her "prize problem student". Of course her efforts bombed big time!

The use of visual strategies does not "cure" anyone, but it frequently simplifies life.

If you try to use a visual tool and it doesn't work, don't scrap the whole system. Look for what may need to be modified to make it work better. I have had teachers show me aids that they have spent considerable time putting together. When I asked, "will the student understand that?", they responded "no". They knew right away that something was not right.

Once you embrace the concept of visual communication supports, envisioning the potential can be both exciting and overwhelming. The temptation may be to try to do too much all at once. Establishing a plan will help. It can take a year to set up the various pieces in a classroom environment. After the basics are established, additions, modifications and revisions will be an ongoing process.

Do you have any additional suggestions to enhance my classroom?

Watch for opportunities to add a visual element to all your standard classroom activities. For music time, add pictures or puppets to represent each of the songs you sing. Support teaching academic skills with lots of visual aids. Each part of the school day has communication demands that can be supported visually. Remember that the communication demands outside the classroom are just as critical. Frequently the non-teaching situations are most in need of communication support.

I am thinking of lots of ways I can use the visual tools in my classroom.

Your enthusiasm will be rewarded! Just remember that a journey of a thousand miles begins with a single step. Once you begin your journey, you will enjoy many discoveries along the way.

> *The development of visual communication strategies is a technique. It is a process... a means to an end. It is not the goal. The goal is effective communication. The visual aids help achieve that goal.*

THE POINT IS:

Visual tools are like having a tool box full of all kinds of tools like hammers and screw drivers and wrenches. Each one is developed to perform a specific function; each tool serves a purpose. You use some of them regularly. Others are pulled out only for special situations. You have a "basic set" that helps fill most of your needs. Occasionally, something comes up that requires a special tool. Some people have big tool boxes; some have small ones. The master carpenter is good at what he does because he has the right tools to work with. Things don't work as well for the weekend handyman who tries to accomplish all his chores with a hammer and a saw.

Including visual tools into a student's communication program works the same way. Some students benefit from more support than others. Many students perform fine with the basics. Other students require more specially designed resources. The master carpenter (the teacher) needs to continually make decisions about what will create the most supportive environment for learning. The ultimate goal is to be sensitive to the student's skills and needs and then provide the supports that will produce the best results. It is an ongoing process.

Part 5

IMPLICATIONS FOR PROGRAMMING

Chapter 11

Educational Trends: Implications For Visually Mediated Communication

Special Education has traversed endless peaks and valleys during its evolutionary journey. Many years ago, individuals with special needs-those who learned differently-were often relegated to life as secondary citizens. Current educational philosophies recognize these people *can* learn. While there is agreement that all students should benefit from educational support, there occurs a wide range of philosophy about educational objectives. Successful outcomes depend on what and how students are taught and how they are able to integrate that learning into functional, independent life participation.

The current trend to identify educational outcomes puts educators under scrutiny. Teaching for teaching sake is not enough. There is an obligation to target goals and move students toward accomplishing those goals. From the days of the one room schoolhouse, educators have continued to develop a more sophisticated understanding of the nature of learning and the many variations of learning style demonstrated by students. This discovery has led us to identify even more students who don't learn effectively when exposed to the more "traditional" teaching styles. It has created ongoing discoveries about the effectiveness of teaching techniques and the provision of support services.

More "educational handicaps" have been identified and the populations of special education caseloads have increased in the last number of years. Development of effective communication skills has been targeted as a core element of educational need. While regular education has approached teaching with traditional methods, we keep identifying more students who learn differently. Their learning differences are significant in both style and quantity. Special educators have been striving toward the development of specialized, individualized teaching strategies, aimed toward teaching skills in a meaningful context. The result has been the creation of a greater variety of teaching techniques that produce more effective learning environments, not only for the students with special needs, but for other students as well. The development of visually mediated communication strategies is one of those techniques that has wide application.

Educational philosophy continues to evolve as we learn more. It is affected, not only by scientific and medical discoveries, but by social opinions, community desires and budgetary constraints. The pendulum keeps swinging back and forth between isolating students with special needs for targeted training or including them with the rest of the regular education population and attempting to meet their individual needs in that environment. These environmental options suggest different intensities of individual attention and different proportions of individual versus group goals. While riding that pendulum, it is important to recognize that each educational setting offers valuable elements. The goal should be to maximize those elements that are most important for each student's individual success.

Use of visual communication strategies fits neatly into this educational see-saw. Visual supports adapt to any environment. It is fairly easy to implement the ideas discussed here for the benefit of the students in any classroom. Then, as the student with special needs is accommodated for, he is not singled out to be totally different from others. As students with special needs are assimilated into regular education environments, questions arise related to their ability to function independently. Questions arise about how much and what kind of support to provide for success. Visual tools provide more normalization than some of the other options.

Despite the philosophical evolution, current state-of-the art thinking suggests students with moderate to severe communication handicaps need to be taught functional skills, aiming toward as much independence as they are capable of as adults. Visual communication strategies support that goal.

WHAT ARE THE QUESTIONS?

When Visually Mediated Communication has been introduced to educators and caregivers, a number of questions and concerns have been expressed. These comments have highlighted how using this system suggests some thinking that varies from traditional teaching techniques. Here are some of the concerns.

THE SKEPTIC SAYS:
"He understands everything I say. He is just being bad."
In reality, many of these students don't understand everything we say. They pick up cues from the routine, the context of the situation, the gestures and facial expressions we use, and other clues to help them guess how they are to respond. It is important for us to recognize what cues are giving them the most information so we can structure the environment to accommodate for that.

The group of students who exhibit difficulty focusing their attention may well understand the language, but their problem lies more in their ability to focus long enough to absorb what they need to absorb and then follow through to completion. Visual strategies provide support in their area of need.

THE SKEPTIC SAYS:
"But this isn't teaching SPEECH!"
Depending on their training and orientation, some Speech-Language Pathologists feel the focus on the development of visual communication supports is outside of their domain. A broader view acknowledges speech, articulation or language structure as only a portion of the "comprehensive communication system" a student needs for effective functioning. Developing an efficient and effective communication system is the real goal. That system should emphasize a variety of elements that work together.

THE SKEPTIC SAYS:
"But this is teaching SPEECH...I am the classroom teacher and that's not my job! It's the job of the Speech-Language Pathologist"
The truth is, communication (including speech if the student has that skill) is the foundation of all other learning a student does. It is important to consider the development of communication skills as an integrated part of the student's total learning program.

THE SKEPTIC SAYS:
"But I have too many other things to teach!"
Communication is the foundation on which all other learning is built. Having an adequate communication environment will enhance any other teaching goals. Both therapists and classroom teachers will experience more success with their other teaching goals if communication goals are given primary importance.

THE SKEPTIC SAYS:
"Shouldn't we be teaching them better auditory skills?"
It is important to teach students to be attentive listeners, however for many of them, "cure" is not a realistic goal. An auditory or attention problem is a part of their handicap; that may always be there. Giving them ways to support or compensate for their areas of difficulty are valuable teaching goals.

THE SKEPTIC SAYS:
"No one is going to do all this visual stuff later, so why should I do it now?"
It is important to develop systems that will help a student perform most effectively now. By structuring current learning environments, their learning rates will be enhanced. A goal when students move into different school, work, and living environments is to communicate with future caregivers what systems have been most successful for them. Students who will move into more independent environments will benefit from having learned techniques that they can continue to use to give themselves support.

THE SKEPTIC SAYS:
"Won't they just depend on pictures?"
Visual tools are designed to help students perform better. If the pictures are meaningful to them and help them be more successful, why should that be a problem? Using pictures or any other visual form does not "take away" skill from the student...it should serve to enhance his participation.

Some students who can read prefer pictures for immediate recognition. They think using pictures is easier. The type of symbols used should match student preference and most successful performance. After all, the advertising world bombards us all with pictures.

THE SKEPTIC SAYS:
"He already knows how to (sign...talk...etc.) Using visual tools will be a step backward"
Observation of numerous students exposed to these tools has revealed that most students benefit from some forms of visual tools. Remember the primary purpose of using visual tools is to enhance student's receptive skills. Even if a student has an effective expressive means, the visual tools serve to enhance his receptive and organizational communication. Visual tools may also supplement or help expand his expressive communication in specific situations. Visual supports can enhance anyone's communication system.

THE SKEPTIC SAYS:

"He is too high skilled." "He is too low skilled."
Students with special needs are never too high skilled to benefit from some visual tools. The format should adjust to meet individual needs and preferences.

It has been encouraging to observe some lower skilled students acquire an understanding of a small but significant number of pictures of highly desired objects or events...particularly those used for giving information to the student. Remember visual strategies include more than just pictures. The success appears to be directly related to the specific items selected and the training procedures used. There is some relationship between the student's ability level and the speed with which he learns to recognize visual stimuli.

THE SKEPTIC SAYS:

"You seem to have an answer for all my questions."
Although some people have related initial questions about the use of visual tools to mediate communication, observing the success of the systems has created an enthusiasm for their use. Once people understand the goal of visually mediated communication, they begin to think of increasingly more ways that can enhance environments visually.

The questions have answers. What is most important, however, are the results. Those who have implemented these strategies have been encouraged to do more. Student performance has alleviated the concerns.

THE ROLE OF
THE CLASSROOM TEACHER

Who is the classroom teacher? A person whose goal is to educate students. How that is done depends on what school he attended to receive his teacher education and when he went to school. It depends on the curriculum in the school where she teaches. It depends on the subjects he teaches or the kind of classroom she has. Add to these factors the teaching experiences the teacher has already had and the current classroom grouping. Many factors come together to define the classroom teacher's style and direction. Just like the students, each teacher is an individual.

The field of education is a dynamic one. Educational philosophies change and someone is always demanding one more thing to teach. As school organization is modified there is always one more thing to be responsible for. Add to this a Speech-Language Pathologist who wants to change things. Depending on what kind of a day you have had, you may receive this news with open arms or with your heels dug in.

What we do know is that as professionals we have learned a lot about what makes sense for students. We know more about what they need to learn and how they need to learn it. That knowledge does not answer all the questions or provide all the answers. What it does is steer us in a direction.

There are so many variables. The effectiveness of the classroom teacher's efforts depends on "doing what you can with what you have to work with." Ideally, these visual communication strategies will add to your efforts to develop meaningful classroom programming. Be open to the possibilities. If you are a "more experienced" educator, recognize that there are many changes currently occurring in philosophy and technique related to the development of communication. If you are a more recently trained educator, recognize that your training has only begun.

The most productive results frequently come from collaboration. Ideally, your support staff will be able to work together with you to "tread some new waters" and "explore some uncharted territory." The more effectively you are able to let them know what kinds of support will be most meaningful to you and the more you are able to collaborate for a common goal, the more satisfying the results will be. Combining efforts can provide an adventure that will be fruitful and successful.

THE EVOLVING ROLE OF THE SPEECH-LANGUAGE PATHOLOGIST

The field of Speech-Language Pathology has undergone continuous metamorphosis as the definition of communication and the scope of communication training has broadened. There has been a transition of thinking. Experience has demonstrated that the traditional "medical model" of training, emphasizing episodic, pullout, isolated skill training, has not consistently produced desired results. That model is based on a goal of remediation to eliminate problems.

Students who experience moderate to severe communication disorders are not easily "fixed". Their needs are more global than an isolated skill deficit. Their communication needs define their overall learning style. Consequently, there has been a shift in the goal of intervention. Professionals are emersed in a change of focus away from teaching isolated speech and language skills in structured, out of context settings. The trend has been to teach functional skills, integrating training into natural, functionally relevant, environments. It is now understood that communication skills need to be taught in rich, interactive environments that provide natural opportunities for skill building. In addition, there is a growing recognition of the need of many students to focus more attention on the *receptive* component of the communication process.

Author's note:
*Considering this discussion of visual strategies, I wish my job title was not Speech Therapist or Speech-Language Pathologist. I would rather be called a Communication Specialist. I would like to change the title of the service I provide from Speech Therapy to Communication Training. These changes would give scope and a more accurate expectation to the services provided for students. They would also have tremendous implications for long term goals developed for students. Replacing the word **speech** with the word **communication** gives a broader domain into which my professional knowledge and skills can have impact.*

Historically, therapists have been faced with some often arbitrary and outmoded institutional constraints regarding when and how and where they can provide service for their students. At the same time, many classroom teachers were raised under the theory that "speech" or "communication" training was the responsibility of the Speech-Language Pathologist. Consequently, it wasn't specifically included as a part of the classroom routine. Fortunately that is changing. Therapists and teachers are exploring new ways to develop collaborative and consultative forms of service to better meet the needs of identified students.

The current trend that is unfolding recognizes the need to allow Speech-Language Pathologists to leave their private rooms and enter the classrooms and environments where real student communication occurs. This has opened numerous opportunities for them to utilize their knowledge and expertise to impact student learning. This change of environments enables therapists and classroom teachers to learn different ways of working together for the student's benefit. One result of this newfound interchange is the development of highly effective learning environments where the training of communication skills is thoroughly integrated into ongoing programming. This emphasizes the training of effective communication skills to be a foundation for overall learning in the educational environment.

The communication tools in this book suggest a different focus and approach to training communication skills than is common in many school environments. Utilizing these ideas encourages collaboration between Speech-Language Pathologists and classroom teachers. In fact, it is in that collaborative process that productive, creative problem solving and programming flourishes.

For the Speech-Language Pathologist, participating in the development of Visual Communication Tools can be a significant contribution in servicing students. In order to focus on this type of support, it may be necessary for the therapist to alter the way services are delivered for a particular student's benefit. Less time may be spent on "direct therapy" and more time spent with activities such as analyzing environments and consulting with teachers and other caregivers. Flexibility is the key to providing the best service. Flexibility means giving the therapist permission to use available time to perform whatever needs to be done to develop a student's program.

Services the Speech-Language Pathologist provides could include
supports such as:

Evaluation:

- ❏ Interview teachers, parents and other caregivers about the
  student's communication performance
- ❏ Analyze the environments where the student functions
- ❏ Observe the student's communication performance in classroom
  and out-of-classroom environments
- ❏ Identify specific communication needs and functional daily
  problems to be supported through better communication
  strategies

Planning:

- ❏ Guide selection of communication objectives
- ❏ Participate in development of the plan to meet objectives

Implementation:

- ❏ Work with classroom staff to develop environmental changes to
  support student learning
- ❏ Help develop classroom routines that create opportunities to
  support better student participation and to practice targeted
  communication skills
- ❏ Collaborate in designing Visual Communication Tools to support
  student functioning
- ❏ Cooperative teaching with classroom staff to support student
  skill development
- ❏ Monitor individual student's programs and progress

These functions are not all inclusive. They are listed merely to suggest
the breadth of activities that may be a necessary part of effectively
developing a system of visual supports. It is critical to remember that
identifying a need or making a visual tool is just one small step in the
process of developing an integrated training program. The therapist
should not be relegated to "cut & paste" duties or the role of an
isolationist, but rather provide an important body of knowledge to a
team effort. The collaborative and consultation approaches broaden the
support for the student's overall learning. The therapist is an essential
part of that team.

PUTTING IT ALL TOGETHER

Students who experience moderate to severe communication disabilities face significant challenges. Communication is the essence of interpersonal relationships. It is the foundation for learning.

As educators tackle the issue of how to educate these students, they sometimes experience philosophical collisions. This represents the "growing pains" of discovery. The goal is to keep growing...keep learning ...keep broadening the range of what we understand and what we do until it fully meets the need. Growing is risky business. Think of the creative chef...combining what is known to be good food into different combinations and adding seasonings to create a new dish. Of course, there are some flops along the way, but learning what does not work leads us to what does work. Often the smallest touches-or a delicate balance-can produce a creation *par excellence*.

The concepts discussed in this book suggest immersing in that same creative exploration. It does not encourage-as some fads do-throwing out everything from the past. Rather it suggests selecting quality ingredients and building upon them. The principles that encourage the implementation of visual strategies are ingredients. Like the chef's seasonings and spices, they can work independently or combine with other elements to produce desired results. Focusing on the receptive part of the communication circle and enhancing the visual component in the communication environment will create positive differences. It is like comparing the cuisine of the fast food hamburger flipper with the delicacies produced by the trained French chef. They are not the same.

The use of visual strategies has moved from the "incidental" category to a designation of "critically important". It has moved from an "afterthought" to the designation of "foundation stone." Once that direction is established, the ideas will flourish.

APPENDIX

Footnotes

1. Courchene, 1991.

2. Prizant & Schuler, 1987.

3. Quill, 1995.

4. Prizant & Schuler, 1987.

5. Mehrabian, 1972.

References and Additional Reading

Carr, E. (1985). Behavioral approaches to communication in autism. In E. Schopler & G. Mesibov (Eds.), *Communication problems in autism.* New York: Plenum Press.

Courchene, E. (1991). A new model of brain and behavior development in infantile autism. *Autism Society of America Conference Proceedings.* Indianapolis, IN: ASA.

Bondy, A., & Frost, L. (1994). The picture exchange communication system. *Focus on Autistic Behavior,* 9(3), 1-19.

Frith, U. (1989). *Autism, explaining the enigma.* Worcester, England: Billings.

Grandin, T. (1990). Needs of high functioning teenagers and adults with autism. *Focus on Autistic Behavior,* 5(1), 1-16.

Grandin, T. (1991). Autistic perceptions of the world. *Autism Society of America Conference Proceedings.* (pp. 85-94). Indianapolis, IN: ASA.

Gray, C. A., & Garand, J. D. (1993). Social stories: Improving responses of students with autism with accurate social information. *Focus on Autistic Behavior,* 8(1), 1-10.

Grofer, L. (1990). Helping the child with autism to understand transitions. *The Advocate,* 21 (4).

Hodgdon, L. (1991). Solving behavior problems through better communication strategies. *Autism Society of America Conference Proceedings* (pp. 212-214). Indianapolis, IN: ASA.

Hodgdon, L. (1995). Solving social - behavioral problems through the use of visually supported communication. In K. Quill (Ed.), *Teaching children with autism.* Albany: Delmar Publishing Co.

Kistner, J., Robbins, F., & Haskett, M. (1988). Assessment and skill remediation of hyperlexic children. *Journal of Autism and Developmental Disorders,* 18, 191-205.

LaVigna, G. (1977). Communication training in mute autistic adolescents using the written word. *Journal of Autism and Childhood Schizophrenia,* 7, 135-149.

LaVigna, G., & Donnellan, A. (1986). *Alternatives to punishment: Solving behavior problems with non-aversive strategies.* New York: Irvington.

Mayer-Johnson, R. (1981). *The picture communication symbols book.* Solana Beach, CA: Mayer-Johnson Co.

Mehrabian, A. (1972). *Nonverbal communication.* Chicago: Adline Publishing Co.

Mirenda, P., & Iacono, T. (1988). Communication options for persons with severe and profound disabilities: State of the art and future directions. *Journal of the Association for Persons with Severe Handicaps,* 15, 3-21.

Mirenda, P., & Santogrossi, J. (1985). A prompt-free strategy to teach pictorial communication system use. *Augmentative and Alternative Communication,* 1, 143-150.

Orelove, F.P. (1982). Developing daily schedules for classrooms of severely handicapped students. *Education and Treatment of Children,* 5, 59-68.

Paul, R. (1987). Communication. In D. Cohen & A. Donnellan (Eds.) *Handbook of autism and pervasive developmental disorder.* New York: John Wiley.

Pierce, K., & Schreibman, L. (1994). Teaching daily living skills to children with autism in unsupervised settings through pictorial self-management. *Journal of Applied Behavior Analysis,* 27 471-481.

Prior, M. (1979). Cognitive abilities and disabilities in autism: A review. *Journal of Abnormal Child Psychology,* 2, 357-380.

Prizant, B. (1983). Language and communication in autism: Toward an understanding of the "whole" of it. *Journal of Speech and Hearing Disorders,* 48, 296-307.

Prizant, B. & Schuler, A. (1987). Facilitating communication: Language approaches. In D. Cohen & A. Donnellan (Eds.) *Handbook of autism and pervasive developmental disorder.* New York: John Wiley.

Quill, K. (1991). Methods to enhance student learning, communication and self-control. *Autism Society of America Conference Proceedings.* Indianapolis, IN: ASA.

Quill, K. (1995). *Teaching children with autism: strategies to enhance communication and socialization.* Albany, NY: Delmar Publishing Co.

Rogers, S. J., & Lewis, H. (1989). An effective day treatment model for young children with pervasive developmental disorders. *Journal of the American Academy of Child and Adolescent Psychiatry,* 28, 207-214.

Rotholz, D., & Berkowitz, S. (1989). Functionality of two modes of communication in the community by students with developmental disabilities: A comparison of signing and communication books. *Journal of the Association for Persons with Severe Handicaps,* 14, 227-233.

Smith, M. (1990). *Autism and life in the community: Successful interventions for behavioral challenges.* Baltimore: Brookes.

Vygotsky, L. S. (1987). *Mind in society: The development of higher psychological processes.* Cambridge: Harvard University Press.

Whitehouse, J., & Harris, J. (1984). Hyperlexia in infantile autism. *Journal of Autism and Developmental Disorders,* 14, 281-290.

Williams, D. (1992). *Nobody nowhere.* New York: Times Books.

Wing, L. (1988). The continuum of autistic characteristics. In E. Schoper & G. Mesibov (Eds.) *Diagnosis and assessment.* New York: Plenum.

About The Author

Linda Hodgdon has been addressing the communication needs of students diagnosed as Autistic, Behavior Disordered, and Severely Language Impaired for over twenty-five years. Her leadership has developed a program model for enhancing the development of communication that has been emulated in districts across the state of Michigan. This program has emphasized the integration of communication training into ongoing functional activities and the development of visually supported communication systems. Hodgdon's work was acknowledged when the Macomb Autistic Program was designated "Program of the Year" by the Michigan Speech and Hearing Association.

A sought after speaker, Linda Hodgdon shares her expertise through frequent consultation, conference presentations, school inservices, and as an instructor for university programs. Her programs are packed with lots of practical information and ideas for improving communication for students who experience communication disorders.

Exciting News!

Volume II of Visual Strategies for Improving Communication is already in progress. Do you have any questions or comments to be addressed? How about some success stories, samples, or challenges that you have faced? Please send your communications to the publisher:

QuirkRoberts Publishing
P.O. Box 71
Troy, MI 48099-0071